Advance Praise for *The Story of Our Time*

Good news! For all the divisive shadows rising across the landscape of the global community these days, there is an answering and much more potent luminosity. Human consciousness is unfolding toward its essential unity – not only with other humans but also with all Life. This lucid book both celebrates that evolutionary trajectory and guides our full and empowered participation.

-**Mirabai Starr**, author of *Caravan of No Despair: A Memoir of Loss & Transformation*, and *God of Love: A Guide to the Heart of Judaism, Christianity & Islam*

What makes this book a classic is its profound stretch across the philosophical, metaphysical, scientific, and spiritual panorama of existence, all wrapped in the universal language of connectivity that unites all sentient beings: Love. It is a must-read by the widest of global audiences.

-**Michael Bernard Beckwith**, author of *Life Visioning*

This beautiful book helps us find a whole new category of understanding evolution. It is not a materialistic process seen only from the outside; it is the interior journey of humanity's consciousness, love and creativity, a remarkable work that I recommend wholeheartedly.

-**Barbara Marx Hubbard**, author of *Conscious Evolution: Awakening the Power of Our Social Potential*

As Muhammad said, "To every age its own book." Atkinson's *The Story of Our Time* aptly summarizes today's story of emergent conscious unity across our species. Organizing the scientific, spiritual, and myriad other elements of this story into seven binding principles only further enhances the value of this book.

-**Kurt Johnson**, organizer of The Interspiritual Network, and author of
The Coming Interspiritual Age

With clarity and insight, Atkinson describes this pivotal moment in our collective evolution. Here are the guidelines for the shift in consciousness humanity needs to make if we are to survive and transform, if we are to make the transition from "the love of power to the power of love." Here is real hope grounded in the deep understanding of life's essential unity and our innate capacity for love.

-**Llewellyn Vaughan-Lee**, Sufi teacher and author of *Spiritual Ecology: The Cry of the Earth*

In *The Story of Our Time,* Robert Atkinson bravely, audaciously, and compellingly identifies factors that can move the consciousness of humanity toward the unity that underlies the divisions of ordinary perception – and, as he astutely illustrates, there is no greater task before us. This is an important contribution to the evolutionary dialogue that is our best hope of transcending the problems that our constricted awareness has created.

-**Philip Goldberg**, author of *American Veda: From Emerson and the Beatles to Yoga and Meditation, How Indian Spirituality Changed the West*

Robert Atkinson's *The Story of Our Time* is a thoughtful, balanced, and gracious contribution from the Baha'i perspective, introducing a stream of unitive evolutionary wisdom that has been ahead of the curve for a long time and deserves to be more widely known.

-**Cynthia Bourgeault**, author of *The Wisdom Way of Knowing; The Holy Trinity and the Law of Three*; and, *The Heart of Centering Prayer: Nondual Christianity in Theory and Practice*

In our western cultures we have developed an obsession with ego, self, individuality, and personhood, and have neglected the collective, unitary aspects that bind all of life into an integral whole. This has led to an unbalanced focus on exploitation, selfishness, and greed, which now threaten our very existence. Individuality is wonderful and necessary, but only in relationship to unity and wholeness. Our future as a species depends on our recognition of this inescapable fact. Although our situation is urgent and time is not on our side, doom and gloom are inappropriate. Rather, hope and love and optimism can see us through, as Robert Atkinson shows in his magnificent *The Story of Our Time*. Consider Atkinson's book as a survival manual, and spread it as widely as possible.

-**Larry Dossey**, MD, author of *One Mind: How Our Individual Mind Is Part of a Greater Consciousness and Why It Matters*

We humans are meaning makers, and our primary vehicle for meaning making is story telling. What we need most desperately today is a new story reflecting the interdependence of all reality. Robert Atkinson's *The Story of Our Time* is a powerful call for creating that new story. I urge you to heed it.

-**Rami Shapiro**, author of *Perennial Wisdom for the Spiritually Independent*

Congratulations on presenting us with a beautifully choreographed prayer with words that gracefully guides us on a path toward resolution of the confounding forces escalating in these times. These are the themes I strive to express through traditional Indigenous music and dance.... well done!

-**Kevin Locke**, Lakota Hoop Dancer, Northern Plains flute player, storyteller, educator, and National Heritage Fellow

As I read through Atkinson's original and timely book, I am saying, 'yes, yes, yes!" Spiritually profound and mentally challenging, *The Story of Our Time* offers a clear solution to the angry divisiveness of today's world.

Atkinson proposes that all of humanity is connected at the core level, with love as the inherent force. He notes that a global transformation is currently under way, creating a shift in consciousness which will point the way to world peace. This is a significant book that every thinking person needs to read!

-**Rev. Elizabeth Stookey**, Interfaith Chaplain and Creator of One Light, Many Candles Multifaith Program

I recommend this book to anyone wondering about the future of humanity. In it, Bob Atkinson proposes the possibility that instead of moving toward extinction as many feel, we are evolving toward peace, justice, and compassion, and that we can speed along this transformation, the more conscious we become of what we are doing.

-**Lewis Mehl-Madrona**, MD, PhD, author of *Healing the Mind Through the Power of Story*

The Story of Our Time is, I believe, in tune with what is going on in our world; it will be comforting for people to have this framework in the face of the "catastrophes" we are living, in order to better understand them. This book is very relevant to the interfaith/interspiritual community, and it is critical for our energy and sanity that we sacred activists of today know that our work is supported by the rich and inspiring history of the interfaith leaders of yesterday that Atkinson describes with such passion.

-**Jacob Watson**, founder of the Chaplaincy Institute of Maine, and author of *Essence: The Emotional Path to Spirit*, and *Enso Morning: Daily Meditation Gifts*

The Story of Our Time is a most timely tome. Atkinson has taken the pulse of the most important issues of our era and integrates the micro and the macro: from individual consciousness to the oneness of humanity. With eloquence and power he demonstrates the importance of both love and justice, two fundamental ethical and spiritual principles, in the development of human consciousness. He has a fresh take on religion that can satisfy and inform both scientists and the spiritually-minded that have rejected religion. He then leads us down a rational path toward understanding the spiritual forces that are transforming both our planet and our individual minds. He explicates the mighty convergence that heralds the coming of age of humanity: our inherent oneness. This volume is a must-read for anyone concerned with the future of humankind.

-**Rhett Diessner**, Professor of Psychology at Lewis-Clark State College, and author of *Psyche and Eros*

THE STORY OF
OUR TIME

THE STORY OF
OUR TIME

FROM DUALITY
TO INTERCONNECTEDNESS
TO ONENESS

Robert Atkinson

The Story Of Our Time: From Duality To Interconnectedness To Oneness
Robert Atkinson
Tradepaper ISBN: 978-1-945026-23-2
Library of Congress Control Number: 2016955497

Editor: Kate Sheehan Roach
Cover Image: Tamera Cooke
Cover Background Texture: Paree Erica
Published by Sacred Stories Publishing
Delray Beach, FL
www.sacredstoriespublishing.com

Printed in the United States of America

Table of Contents

The pattern of collective evolution

Justice as the cornerstone of an ever-advancing civilization

The polarity principle

The necessity of adversity

The dark night of the collective soul

A world giving birth

Reality as a continuum

Uniting the One and the many

A global transformation of consciousness is under way

Beyond political peace, world unity is the goal

A holistic view of the Creator

Re-visioning religion

The missing chapter in the story of religion

Humanity's coming of age

Prologue

We're Living in a Spiritual Springtime

It's astounding that the entire universe obeys the same fundamental laws of nature. But how could it be any other way? These laws are constant, can be observed, and allow us to identify patterns in all realms of existence, since the physical and spiritual realms are mirror reflections of the same reality.

Patterns like the cycle of seasons, the rise and fall of civilizations, and the cycle of spiritual epochs all share repeating cycles of growth, maturity, decline, and renewal. While we're currently witnessing signs of decline all around us, we're also seeing signs of renewal, since there is an overlap in this process. Decline and renewal are both part of a larger process that holds the promise of rebirth.

Spiritual epochs have clearly punctuated humanity's conscious evolution over the millennia. Spiritual, religious, and social consciousness expands along a continuum, increasing in complexity as our individual and collective development unfolds. Governed by one natural law, a process of maturation followed by decline and eventual renewal is as evident in the realm of religion as it is in individual development, social development, and the cycles of seasons.

It's difficult to deny that the world's major prophets, including Krishna, Abraham, Moses, Zoroaster, Buddha, Jesus, Muhammad, and, Baha'u'llah, founder of the Baha'i Faith in the mid-19th century, have each in their own time impacted the world. Together, they've changed the course of human life over the last four thousand years, bringing about a leap of consciousness with each new epoch they initiated.

Evolution in all realms is tied together, as is becoming more evident every day. We're coming to see that all of Creation is an indivisible oneness, that deep down everything is interconnected, and that all is subject to one law. 20th-century French Jesuit priest-palaeontologist Pierre Teilhard de Chardin puts it this way, "Ultimately, somehow or other there must be only a single energy at play in the world." This awareness stems from the same spiritual foundation as the Baha'i worldview:

> Just as the solar cycle has its four seasons, the cycle of the Sun of Reality has its distinct and successive periods. Each brings its vernal season or springtime. When the Sun of Reality returns to quicken the world of mankind, a divine bounty descends from the heaven of generosity. The realm of thoughts and ideals is set in motion and blessed with new life. Minds are developed, hopes brighten, aspirations become spiritual...It is the springtime of the inner world.

We live in a time of spiritual renewal. A century and three-quarters into the Baha'i Era, we have seen a leap of consciousness from the previous norm of nation-building to the new vision of a global community being built by citizens of the world.

The spiritual energies of the Baha'i Revelation are still in their early days, just beginning to blossom, changing this world into another world. We are the fortunate ones living in the spiritual springtime the Baha'i teachings anticipate. The effects of this budding renewal are being seen and felt everywhere. A global interfaith, interspiritual, indigenous, and interdisciplinary effort is currently bringing people together from all directions, into the cause of oneness.

We live in times of massive change, a necessary element for our inevitable yet precarious progress. Never has there been a greater opportunity–and need–to participate in and take action on behalf of this unfolding process. A renewed commitment to our own spirituality is the only thing that will give us security–personally and collectively–in these changing times.

The most important change is always a change in consciousness. The consciousness characterizing our spiritual epoch that we most need to ensure comes into its summer fullness is the consciousness of the oneness of humanity. Helen Keller challenged the world to embrace this awareness when she asked "When indeed shall we learn that we are all related to one another, that we are all members of one body?" The Baha'i writings focus on just this:

> "World order can be founded only on an unshakeable consciousness
> of the oneness of mankind... all the human sciences recognize only
> one human species, albeit infinitely varied in the secondary aspects of
> life. Recognition of this truth requires abandonment of prejudice—
> prejudice of every kind—race, class, colour, creed, nation, sex, degree
> of material civilization, everything which enables people to consider
> themselves superior to others."

Moving beyond these dualities and toward the oneness that embraces all is the story of our time, our most challenging issue, and the greatest task at hand. This is the movement encircling the globe, engaging the hearts of people everywhere. This is how the entire world is now being renewed in our time.

Introduction

Spiritual Principles Guiding
Our Evolutionary Leap

All matter originates and exists only by virtue of a force. We must assume
behind this force the existence of a conscious and intelligent Mind.

-Max Planck

Faith communities and indigenous cultures worldwide all have core stories addressing the countless mysteries of existence. Many point to a distant time in the future, often seen as the "promised day," or a "great age" of universal harmony when their teachings will be fulfilled. All traditions seem to agree that central to the process of getting there is a much-needed thorough transformation on all levels, from the personal to the collective. The essence of all of these traditions is that there is a built-in need for regular change, transformation, and renewal.

Interestingly, when I was in Guatemala in December of 2012 I spoke with a few Mayans, who still make up 40% of the population there, about the much-hyped end of their Long Count calendar. And each said, matter-of-factly, "The end of one cycle is followed by the beginning of another," confirming a timeless law of nature: progress is always a process of birth, death, and rebirth. Too often, we tend to forget the renewal, or rebirth, part of the process and instead focus only on the death phase.

Yet this is exactly where we stand today—at a critical juncture in our collective evolution. Our time is characterized by rapid change and global crises. And people want answers. Is change random? Is there a direction to evolution? Where is the meaning in all of what we are going through?

All sacred stories about future changes share this universal motif of cyclical transformation within a linear process of progressive evolution. Collective evolution is always a process of expanding consciousness leading to change, growth, and eventually transformation and renewal. This is the story that is repeated over and over again, across the millennia, within all traditions, as chapter 4 explains in more depth.

But the story we have lived with for so long has lost much of its power, and most alarmingly, its hope for the future. Every timeless story brings forth order from chaos, and purpose from conflict; not only does it have a beginning, middle, and an end, but also a beginning, a *muddle*, and a *resolution*. This pattern is found in stories everywhere, from myths to folk tales to our own life stories. When a resolution is achieved, another story begins; and the pattern repeats itself.

The story of our time, of humanity's evolving consciousness, is no different. So far, as 20th-century Catholic priest and ethnohistorian Thomas Berry points out, we have had a difficult time recognizing the evolutionary nature of our sacred story.

Our prevailing story seems to lack a resolution to the *muddle* facing the world today. Missing is the principle of inevitable progress. Swiss psychiatrist C. G. Jung said: "Our myth has become mute, and gives no answers." A myth, in its truest sense a guiding story, needs to be alive and growing, providing inspiration and direction.

Our crisis today is a crisis of consciousness. No longer can we settle only on seeing things in opposition to one another; we need to shift our consciousness to be able to see the parts coming together in a new whole.

A Walk Through Time

A little perspective might help here. Reviewing our common heritage reveals that crises have always been a central part of the history of creation. From a distance, we see that cycles of transformation have always existed, even well before humanity appeared. An organic pattern seems to take us through necessary challenges and crises actually designed to ensure that this process of transformation is ever-advancing.

Thomas Berry identifies four parts to the sacred story of the universe: the galactic story, the Earth story, the story of life, and the human story. A walk through time, starting 4.5 billion years ago at Earth's inception, shows us that the entire human story makes up just 1% of the history of life on Earth. The previous 99% of Earth's history is characterized by crises, as well, yet pre-human history is a cause for celebrating the diversity and continuity of life, *and* a cause for hope.

Imagine the history of life on Earth, in geologic scale, as a one-mile long timeline (4.5 billion years = one mile, which = 1760 yards, or 5280 feet):

4 Billion Years Ago/ 240 Yard Mark (YM)	After forming out of stardust from exploding stars, there is no life on Earth until the first life form, a microscopic, single-celled, anaerobic bacterium appears in the primordial ocean and survives!
950 YM	Beyond the halfway mark, simple species after simple species come and go, until the eukaryote cell, which will eventually come to make up our bodies, evolves.
250 Million Years Ago (MYA)/1660 YM	The greatest mass extinction in Earth's history takes place. 95% of life on Earth disappears, but life picks itself up and continues on, adding even greater diversity.
1662 YM	Giant reptiles appear and last for the next 73 yards (187 million years, very long for any class of animals).
1682 YM	North and South America, Europe, and Africa split and drift apart toward their present locations.

65 MYA/1735 YM	Another disaster occurs; the toxicity stored in the Earth's crust explodes to extinguish 75% of life, including dinosaurs, but setting the stage for the appearance of mammals.
4 MYA/1737 YM	Once again, life picks itself up, resumes its "clean up, diversify, and proliferate" process, and primates appear.
Less than an inch to go	*Homo sapiens* appear, and with us, the beginning of abstract thought, symbols, language, stories, writing, culture, and the evolution of consciousness and spiritual awareness.
10,000 Years Ago/ 1/8th of an inch to go	After hunting and gathering for a half-inch or so, we settled down to become farmers, merchants, and industrialists.
.04 of an inch to go	Buddha was born.
.03 of an inch to go	Jesus was born.
.0006 of an inch to go	Humans split the atom, introducing a threat unprecedented over the entire mile.

From this brief but powerfully humbling story of the evolution of life on earth, we can tell a number of important things:

1. The entire mile of existence is fraught with a series of fits and starts, near-endings, only to be followed by another beginning. The Earth has seen endless repetitions of muddles and resolutions, with *and* without us.
2. Change and evolution are basic to existence, even on its largest scales.
3. Change goes from simplicity and uniformity to increasing complexity

and differentiation. Yet this differentiation is democratic, equal, and universal.

4. Life on this planet is totally transitory, fleeting by nature. It is both linear and cyclical, part of the great circle of life, *and* a gift from the Creator.

5. Equality throughout creation makes it clear as well that a strong underlying unity pervades the universe. Everywhere we look, the same physical laws are at work, the same physical constants apply.

6. Human consciousness, and our entire conscious evolution, happens in less than the final inch of the mile-long walk of life on earth. Though human consciousness is unique in all the realms of creation, it is also connected to and part of all other forms of existence. What became possible in the human mind (the capacity for reflection, awareness of self and others, and the language to communicate these inner musings) was only because of the many advances that had already been made at previous levels of existence.

Finally, the idea of an evolutionary universe becomes much clearer with this walk through the farthest reaches of time, as does the idea that evolution itself took a giant step with the advent of human consciousness. As Brian Swimme put it, "Our ancestry stretches back through the life forms and into the stars, back into the beginnings of the primeval fireball. This universe is a single multiform energetic unfolding of matter, mind, intelligence and life." Indeed, the story of the universe is a sweeping scientific, mythic, and mystical story, and our history has prepared us for our future. But where is the story that will carry us into our desired future?

The Need for a New Chapter in Our Evolving Story

Human consciousness has leapt forward from a localized parochial perspective to an awareness of regional, national, and now international matters. As we approach a consciousness of global integration and interconnectedness, our greatest challenge may be accepting this new, emerging reality, and developing a new story that frames it all. But, as with earlier evolutionary crises, it may be that there are hidden forces guiding this process in which we are necessary participants.

This is the heart of a new chapter in our evolving story that we are gaining greater glimpses of now. As systems theorist Ervin Laszlo points out, what is needed most now is a change in our thinking, a transformation of consciousness, in which "a new worldview with new values adapted to living, surviving, and developing on this planet" would make sense of the past, the present, and a possible future as an on-going evolutionary process because, as he explains, "We are far more interconnected to one another and to all elements than we ever thought."

The story of our interconnectedness is the emerging vision of our time. Yet, its essence has been around for a long time. As the concepts of "the great chain of being" and "the perennial philosophy" have shown, there are principles and values that are shared by all humanity, that are timeless and universal, and that have forever linked all beings and all created phenomena in an interwoven whole.

This expanding worldview also "recognizes a divine Reality substantial to the world of things and lives and minds," as Pierre Teilhard de Chardin put it in explaining his idea that as evolution increases in complexity, an increase in reflective consciousness follows, or that consciousness itself is progressive and ever-advancing, which is the main theme of this book.

A Piece of My Story

Before getting too far, it might be helpful to provide a personal context for where all of this is coming from. It seems I have always known I was part of something much greater than myself. I was drawn from an early age to the mysteries of a reality I could not yet begin to fathom. I became a reflective thinker long before I knew what that meant; at an early age, the consciousness of my soul far exceeded that of my mind.

Growing up around the potato fields, woods, and waters of eastern Long Island as an only child, I was drawn to take regular walks in the woods near my home. I remember these as special times that put me in touch with a living universe. There was something about the woods, the stream, the trees, their leaves, and all of nature that sang of union and heralded a call to adventure each time I entered their realm.

At age nine, when my grandmother came to stay with us, I became fascinated by her commitment to her spiritual life. She read daily from *The Bible* and *The Upper Room*. Something inside my nine-year-old mind, or heart, wanted to know more about what I couldn't grasp, what gave her such a sense of devotion. I didn't know it then, but what I observed from my grandmother made a difference to my soul.

Around this time, while sitting on my bed looking out the window, a "voice" came to me saying, "Someday *you* will know God." Years later, I realized this was a metaphor, as I've come to understand the supreme force of the universe as the unknowable Essence, though the manifestations of its bounty are evident everywhere.

My life was telling a story before I knew it. Parades of celebration filled the streets the day I was born, my mother told me. Not for me, but for the first atomic bomb that turned a world at war into a nuclear village. My life had become a subtle quest to find an elusive peace.

I did the usual things during my childhood and adolescence—sports, hanging out with the right crowds – but was mostly unaware of who I was or where I was going. It was almost as if I was sleepwalking through those years.

In college, I majored in philosophy and my investigation of reality began in earnest. Eastern and western philosophers, as well as the world's religions, captured my attention and became my passion.

After completing a master's degree in American Folk Culture, a series of adventures led me from one remarkable event to another in the summer of 1969. From watching the moonwalk, to sailing on the maiden voyage of the Hudson River sloop *Clearwater* from New York to Albany with Pete Seeger, my first mentor, which included a few sloop festivals along the way, we got to Albany just in time for a few of us to attend the big festival at Woodstock.

That fall, living in a small cabin in the woods by the river, I deepened my study of the world's religions and further explored the cycles of nature in the woods around me.

I stayed as a guest in a nearby Franciscan monastery that winter, and on a visit to New York City one evening, while looking in the 8th Street Bookshop window, a book on mythology caught my eye. Inside, after paging through the book for a while, I looked up at a poster on the bulletin board and discovered that Joseph Campbell, whose book I was reading, was giving a lecture that evening at Cooper Union, a few blocks away. With minutes to spare, I walked right over there.

Sitting front and center in the Great Hall, a huge crowd filed in all around me, and I listened intently to every word he said. As if I were the only one in the hall, he described the mythic journey in a way that mirrored perfectly my own experiences at the time. Afterwards, I introduced myself, and told him how much what he had to say meant to me. He responded very warmly and encouragingly. We kept in touch, and I visited him in his Greenwich Village home a couple of times.

On one of those visits, he gave me a signed copy of *The Masks of God: Creative Mythology*, the final volume in a series, in which he wrote that the series confirmed for him "a thought I have long and faithfully entertained: of the unity of the human race, not only in its biology but also in its spiritual history which has everywhere unfolded in the manner of a single symphony, with its themes…irresistibly advancing to some kind of mighty climax." He became a second key mentor for me, providing a vision that has become the centerpiece of my own worldview.

A while after this, my ongoing study of the world's religions found fulfillment in the common core of spiritual principles, wholeness, and unity expressed so beautifully in the writings of Baha'u'llah, the 19th-century founder of the Baha'i Faith.

This period in my life provided the settings and circumstances for my memoir, *Remembering 1969: Searching for the Eternal in Changing Times*, chronicling a journey of soul-making that connected me to the universal layer of my existence, a timeless pattern countless others have lived, and a universal story told so often. I've come to see all of this as an openness to the mysteries around us as that lead us into a deeper understanding of ourselves and a deeper connection to others. These are the experiences and the perspective through which I have come to view all things.

After earning a doctorate in cross-cultural human development, I taught the human development and culture and diversity courses for the counselor education program at the University of Southern Maine for twenty-seven years. Knowing that the human life cycle includes the journey of the soul and that diversity is the nature of life—the goal of which is realizing the highest possible degree of unity in diversity—a sense of wholeness and interconnectedness has been the underlying theme of my life.

Timeless Principles to Guide Us

That there are underlying principles to help us better understand the nature of evolution should also help restore some of our faith in the future. Understanding things on the level of principles gives us a much better chance of finding answers to the perplexing questions of purpose, direction, and outcomes. This is why both science *and* religion are central players in the story of the evolution of consciousness.

And this is also why I have taken a principle-centered approach here to explore the nature of consciousness, the nature of transformation, and the nature of Reality. The seven principles framing and helping to demystify these concepts are:

1. *Consciousness is a potentiality set in motion by an organic process.* Now more than ever, the independent investigation of reality will unleash our full potential.
2. *Love is the underlying force of evolution.* Love is an inherent unifying force meant to evolve personal and collective potential to its highest degree.
3. *Justice maintains the inherent balance of life.* Equitable and just relationships on all levels evolve with the increase of social complexity over time.
4. *Unity is the result of the conscious confrontation of opposing forces.* The merging of opposites, through transformation, is necessary for growth and evolution.
5. *Reality is one, and global harmony is inevitable.* World peace is a promise waiting to be fulfilled; how we get there is up to us to determine.
6. *Revelation is continuous and progressive.* The release of spiritual energies always has been, and will be, the inspiration for the evolution of civilization.

7. *Consciousness evolves toward wholeness and unity.* Science and religion, two knowledge systems within the same whole, cannot be in opposition.

These seven principles, further supported by the eight precepts described in chapter 6, imply one animating force governing both a linear and cyclical process of transformation regulating our evolutionary march onward. As the world's sacred texts and classic and leading-edge thinkers alike tell us, the essence of these principles is that the need to change, grow, and evolve is the nature of life; the nature of life is to provide a basic opposition *by which* we grow and evolve; and, the nature of this basic opposition in life is to bring about transformation, which ensures progress.

These seven principles break down a timeless pattern of evolution, which is guided by a force leading us toward the recognition of our intended oneness. They've been derived from the Baha'i teachings and are supported by the mystical traditions of Judaism, Christianity, and Islam, as well as various indigenous teachings, Hinduism, Zoroastrianism, and Buddhism. They provide a framework for a new story of our time centered upon the idea of the evolution of religion itself.

While distilled here to their essence, and serving as the skeletal structure of this book, a more developed explanation of each principle appears as a preface to each chapter. These principles are meant to serve as the bones into which we can each breathe our own breath of life as co-creators of a new story of human conscious evolution. This is a story that needs us as much as we need it. Without it, our very existence is threatened. With it, evolution will march onward toward its fulfillment.

Definitions for a few of the key terms used in the book might be helpful here. Reality, or Ultimate Reality, refers to the transcendent power and goodness that both created and directs the entire creation. While given various names by the world's sacred traditions, this higher Reality is both beyond and within us, but exceeds the reach of our earthly language, while linking us to the oneness of creation. Ultimate Reality is both personal (an active, beneficent Creator) and non-personal (the Transcendent, Absolute, divine Principle or Power), and even more, it is all-inclusive.

Opening up to this Reality initiates the process of our own awakening to the realization of our deeper identity as a reflection of this Reality. All paths that include this quality of openness, expectation, and trust lead us closer to the ultimate mystery we seek, and into a universal experience of knowing something more than what is visible. This experience of unity with what is beyond us satiates our hunger even more for the infinite, causing us to value our relationship with Reality more than anything.

Reality is thus seen as changeless, though consciousness itself changes and evolves, and is understood as *the entirety of existence which is an interconnected whole with one common source, and one guiding force, but whose essence is unknowable.*

The term "principle" is used here, from *principium*, as an essential truth, a *tenet, precept, or truism that explains a natural action or order in the make-up of Reality.*

Consciousness, here, deals with the "upper" limits of potential, where love and justice reside, rather than with questions of its existence at its "lower" limits, and is seen as both: *the level or degree of awareness we have of reality,* and *the capacity we have to reflect on and make greater sense of personal and transpersonal experience and reality.*

Transformation is *the process by which personal and collective evolution is not just changed but quickened, altered, and significantly shifted in bringing about an expanded understanding through the merging of opposing forces into a new and unified wholeness.*

Evolution, another key concept, implying long-term order with the possibility of short-term chaos, is used here as *the guiding force of the universe, as well as the process overseeing the progressive growth and development of individuals and society as a whole.*

Underlying all of this is a worldview in which the spiritual dimension is an indispensable component, in conjunction with other perspectives. Integrating the social sciences, humanities, sciences, and the sacred texts of the world's religions to achieve a deeper and fuller understanding of the whole of reality, this book breaks new ground in tracing the common thread of unity evident throughout our evolution and within all of the world's sacred traditions. It attempts to illustrate that the flow of history, at its very essence, is the story of the spiritual evolution of humankind.

In his seminal book of 1999, *The Mystic Heart: Discovering a Universal Spirituality in the World's Religions*, Brother Wayne Teasdale introduced the idea that we are at the dawn of the Interspiritual Age. Characterized by a new set of historical circumstances, this age is bringing about a number of shifts in consciousness: the emergence of ecological awareness and an acknowledgement of the basic fragility of the earth; a recognition of the interdependence of all domains of life and reality; the desire to abandon a militant nationalism; a deeper experience of community between and among the religions; and a growing receptivity to the inner treasures of the world's religions. Together, these are preparing the way for a new interconnected, universal civilization that will draw its inspiration from perennial spiritual and moral insights.

Could it be that humanity's current transformation of consciousness is linked to the radical statement (especially for the mid-1800s), "The earth is but one country, and mankind its citizens," at the heart of the Baha'i revelation?

The qualities characterizing the Interspiritual Age are reflected in the primary spiritual principles of the Baha'i teachings. While most of the world's religions are currently shifting from tribal or national modes of being toward a more holistic sense of the shared values of all spiritual and religious traditions, the Baha'i Faith came into existence in 1844 with a fully developed understanding of the oneness of humanity.

The Baha'i Faith embodies ideals now considered progressive, though at the time of their 19th-century Persian origin were the cause of severe, and still continuing, persecution. In fact, as Shoghi Effendi, Guardian of the Baha'i Faith said in 1935, "The core of religious faith is that mystic feeling which unites Man with God." This is why he also added, "The Baha'i Faith, like all other Divine Religions, is thus fundamentally mystic in character. Its chief goal is the development of the individual and society, through the acquisition of spiritual virtues and powers," foreshadowing Brother Teasdale's "mystic heart" of all religions.

A quick review of history shows that so much has happened since the mid-nineteenth century, from the thousandfold increase in the speed of travel, to the ten-millionfold increase in the speed of communication, to the exponential explosion of knowledge (with a five-hundredfold increase in the number of U.S. patents just since 1844), to the remarkable mushrooming of computation and information technology and its miraculous miniaturization, to the liberation of women, minorities, and slaves, to the universalization of education, to the desire for a universal language, and to the recognition of the need for a world government.

Spiritual evolution since that same time frame has been more like a spiritual *revolution*. The rise of American transcendentalism created the first bridge between Christianity and the Dharmic religions, and inspired the first Parliament of the World's Religions in 1893 in Chicago, where Hinduism was formally introduced to America with Swami Vivekananda's captivating speech, in which he quoted this hymn from his childhood:

> *"As the different streams having their sources in different places all mingle their water in the sea, so, O Lord, the different paths which men take through different tendencies, various though they appear, crooked or straight, all lead to Thee."*

Also introduced to America at this first Parliament were Jainism, Buddhism, the Baha'i Faith, and others previously unknown here. Having a broad and profound impact on attendees and the general public alike, who heard about the first Parliament of the World's Religions from the world press, this auspicious gathering marked the birth of the global interfaith movement.

Indeed, great progress has been made in every realm in the past century and a half, and though we still have a long way to go, we can't help but wonder if this latest release of spiritual energy in our time is a missing piece in understanding the "new set of historical circumstances" that has made this time so ripe for so many shifts in consciousness. After all, it was at that first Parliament of the World's Religions in 1893 that John Henry Barrows noted, "The solemn charge which the Parliament preaches to all true believers is a return to the primitive unity of the world...The results may be far off, but they are certain."

One of the results of the technological advances of our time that also helped to initiate such a leap of consciousness were the photographs of the Earth sent back to us from the NASA Apollo missions. Space travel inspired astronaut Edgar Mitchell to found the Institute of Noetic Sciences, a nonprofit organization dedicated to supporting individual and collective transformation through consciousness research. The whole world was impacted by the photographs the Apollo astronauts took from space. There are no boundaries between nations in those compelling images; for the first time, we could literally *see* the world as one.

This is the backdrop—and thesis—of this book, as detailed further in chapter three: after having started out in small, isolated homogeneous communities living with a consciousness of oneness, and followed by millennia of diverse communities and nations living at odds with one another with an adopted consciousness of duality, humanity is now beginning to see its common heritage, needs, and goals more clearly, and is attempting to reclaim its consciousness of oneness.

The seven principles framing this book are guiding us from a consciousness of duality, in which one part of the whole is always pitted against another, toward a consciousness of oneness, where equality, justice, and compassion prevail. They are the basis for a worldview that is no longer an anomaly but within the reach of—and a matter of conscious choice for—every human being alive today.

So, the story of our time has three interconnected themes: a) we are living in the early phases of a spiritual revolution, a time of renewed spiritual energy that is reforming all things; b) we therefore live in a time of disintegration and integration, a time when the clash of opposing forces are bringing about a transformation of consciousness; and, c) ours is a time when there are

> All things are bound together,
> all things connect.
> Whatever befalls the earth,
> Befalls also the children
> of the earth.
> ~Chief Oren Lyons

forces in operation to assist in this process, re-creating patterns of interaction and relationship, and enabling disparate parts of the whole (who themselves are also assisting in this renewal) to retrieve our heritage of oneness.

Part One

The Nature Of Consciousness

The major problems in the world are the result of the difference between the way nature works and the way people think.

-Gregory Bateson

Learn to see God in the details of your life,
for He is everywhere...
Let nothing disturb you. Let nothing worry you.
Everything is passing away. Only God is changeless. God alone suffices.

-St. Teresa of Avila

Our present world is conditioned by our present mode of consciousness;
only when that consciousness passes from its present dualistic mode
conditioned by time and space will the new creation appear,
which is the eternal reality of which our world is a mirror.

-Bede Griffiths

Principle 1

Consciousness is a potentiality set in motion by an organic process

As biological development is designed to unfold in degrees and stages, transcending its own seeming limits, so too is our evolving consciousness. Yet, even as a divinely endowed capacity for seeing beyond the seen, and understanding beyond the understood, the fulfillment of consciousness is not guaranteed.

The potentiality of consciousness is wholly dependent upon the initiative taken to actively investigate reality. Consciousness expands as greater and greater levels of awareness and comprehension of self, society, the mysteries of life, and the wonders of the universe are explored in their fullest. As the degree of awareness we have of something increases, and as the capacity to reflect upon and make greater sense of it increases, we are led to a comprehension of its place in the greater whole.

Forces are operating to liberate human consciousness from previously restricted stages, propelling it onward in its evolution. Now, more than ever, it is the independent investigation of reality that will unleash our fullest potential, leading to the spiritualization of human consciousness. The awakening of new capacities is bringing with it the recognition of new responsibilities for a collective maturity that are restructuring society.

Be Lost in the Call

Lord, said David, since you do not need us,
why did you create these two worlds?
Reality replied: O prisoner of time,
I was a secret treasure of kindness and generosity,
and I wished this treasure to be known,
so I created a mirror: its shining face, the heart;
its darkened back, the world;
The back would please you if you've never seen the face.
Has anyone ever produced a mirror out of mud and straw?
Yet clean away the mud and straw,
and a mirror might be revealed.
Until the juice ferments a while in the cask,
it isn't wine. If you wish your heart to be bright,
you must do a little work.
My King addressed the soul of my flesh:
You return just as you left.
Where are the traces of my gifts?
We know that alchemy transforms copper into gold.
This Sun doesn't want a crown or robe from God's grace.
He is a hat to a hundred bald men,
a covering for ten who were naked.
Jesus sat humbly on the back of an ass, my child!
How could a zephyr ride an ass?
Spirit, find your way, in seeking lowness like a stream.
Reason, tread the path of selflessness into eternity.
Remember God so much that you are forgotten.
Let the caller and the called disappear;
be lost in the Call.

-Jalal ad-Din Rumi

1

Our Inherent Urge to Understand Reality

Afoot and light-hearted I take to the open road,
Healthy, free, the world before me,
The long brown path leading wherever I choose.

-Walt Whitman

If we have our own why *in life,*
we shall get along with almost any how....

-Friedrich Nietzsche

I get the urge for going
When the meadow grass is a-turning brown...

-Joni Mitchell

We are born into a mystery. For some, the journey of life seems to provide a fairly steady comfort level, whatever may come. For others, there may be a subtle anxiety about life or death, or both, which may or may not change things. For yet others, there may be an unconscious quest moving toward deeper understanding. And for still others, there may be an all-out, conscious quest, or search for truth, directing every aspect of life.

Perhaps hidden somewhere within us all is what Elizabeth Gilbert, in the popular *Eat, Pray, Love,* calls "the itch, the mad and relentless urge to want to understand the workings of existence."

She tells the story of the youth she met in India who had this "urge," having left his family farm in Ireland to find inner peace through yoga in India. After he had returned home, he sat with his father, the lifelong farmer and man of few words, telling him about his spiritual discoveries. The father listened with mild interest, watching the hearth and the fire, smoking his pipe, as the son said excitedly, "Dad, this meditation stuff, it's crucial for peace and serenity. It can really save your life. It teaches you how to quiet your mind."

His father turned to him and said kindly, "I have a quiet mind already, son," and then returned his gaze to the fire.

Who's to know, really, whether the farmer—or anyone else—has somehow gotten to a "quiet mind"? This may be a universal goal, but its opposite—the Buddhist teaching that most of humanity has their eyes so caked shut with the dust of deception that they will never see truth no matter who tries to show it to them—seems to loom fairly large, as well. Perhaps the only thing we can know for sure is whether or not we ourselves have gotten to that cherished goal.

That's why to truly understand this relentless urge, Gilbert says we have to "look for God, like a man with his head on fire looks for water." In this light, the urge is a single-minded quest that nothing could deter us from.

The Call

Rumi tells us "Be lost in the Call." David, in this poem, asks one of the most mystical questions of all: "Why did you create these two worlds?" Reality replies, likening the worlds to the front and back of a mirror, one side shining brightly and the other dark. If we are prisoners of the temporal world, the dark side may suffice; we may not hear the Call anyway to seek the other side. But if we *have* glimpsed the other side, and have seen the shining face, "the soul of my flesh," we are enabled to "tread the path of selflessness into eternity." We are no longer content with only the temporal world; the Call becomes the loudest sound to our ears.

7th-century Vedanta philosopher Shankara said, "When a man follows the way of the world, or the way of the flesh, or the way of tradition (i.e. when he believes in… the letter of the scriptures, as though they were intrinsically sacred), knowledge of Reality cannot arise in him." To seek to know Reality, we have to be open to what is beyond us, to what is greater than what we already know; we have to be open to connecting with something greater than we are. But this is the way it has always been.

One of the very first archetypes, or patterns of inherited, oft-repeated behavior, is the *call to adventure*, or the quest to understand reality. This is a theme as old as story itself; it is ubiquitous to all literature and the most common basis for all plots.

> *The germ of the transcendent life, the spring of the amazing energy which enables the great mystic to arise to freedom, is latent in all of us; an integral part of our humanity.*
> ~Evelyn Underhill

Perhaps hearing the Call is central to our purpose as human beings. Classic mythology, and fairy tales too, are framed by the motif of search. Mythic heroes became heroes—and heroines—*because* they were the original seekers after truth. Though their adventures involved much drama and many overwhelming challenges, as they all must, Odysseus, Gilgamesh, Inanna, Icarus, Daphne, Jonah, Moses, King Arthur, Sleeping Beauty, *Siddhartha*, and countless others lived out a pattern that is not only understood as heroic but as sacred, too.

The archetype of the *call* consists of a quest that always begins with a separation from the familiar ("from the way of the world"), which signals a "departure," and is followed by the quests' fulfillment in the closely related archetypes of "initiation" and "return." This is the three-part pattern Joseph Campbell has identified as the monomyth, or the adventure of the hero.

The meaning of this archetype is the unfolding of destiny; its appearance is the first sign that something of significance is about to happen. There is usually a herald of some kind signaling the coming of this archetype, as in the frog who retrieves the ball from the pond for the princess. This archetype not only marks the beginning of a transformational undertaking, it is, in mystic terms, "the awakening of the self."

Evelyn Underhill characterizes "the mystic type" as the personality who refuses to be satisfied with someone else's experience. Wherever this "urge for going" takes us, it seems this is where we are meant to be going.

All who seek something beyond have one passion in common: pursuing a spiritual quest to find a "way out" or a "way back" to what will "satisfy their craving for absolute truth," which then also constitutes their whole meaning of life. This, of course, leads to not only the awakening of the self, but to a transcendental consciousness that usually involves a vision of the Divine as immanent in the world.

In the Baha'i tradition, Baha'u'llah, answering a query from a Sufi, explains this mystical quest in the familiar and timeless framework of the seven stages of the journey of the soul, beginning with the motif of *The Valley of Search*, as did the 12th-century Persian Sufi Attar. This confirms that the spiritual realities, or the inner verities, of all religions are the same. He says the first characteristics of the valley of search, after taking "leave of self," are patience and perseverance. Other prerequisites of this quest are to "cleanse the heart" and "turn away from [blind] imitation."

It soon becomes evident in this quest that guidance will be provided when most needed, again from *The Valley of Search*: "At every step, aid from the Invisible Realm" is offered; as the intensity of the search grows, union with "the object of [the] quest" is desired. When the Call is answered, it signals the awakening of consciousness, leading to the fulfillment of a potentiality, like a seed growing into fruition.

The Question of Consciousness

Only by our conscious effort can the potential of consciousness be realized. Consciousness is the dynamic unfolding of a systematic awareness of ourselves in relation to others and the world, and how we put this together to make sense of it all. As consciousness evolves, it changes the way we see everything. Everything exists the way it is because of our *awareness* of it as we see it.

Carl Jung sees consciousness as a process that emerges from the depths. Consciousness awakens gradually from childhood throughout life as contents of the unconscious arise to a conscious level. All human beings share a common biology and a common psychological inheritance. He says, "The collective unconscious contains the whole spiritual heritage of mankind's evolution, born anew in the brain structure of every individual." The iceberg-like *capacity* of consciousness causes our *awareness* to widen, deepen, and take on fuller meaning.

Our developing, evolving consciousness helps fulfill our unique purpose of investigating the nature of Reality. All the world's religions and spiritual philosophies stress the importance of cultivating the capacity of consciousness through a practice that aligns us with the universal order.

Consciousness is a complex capacity consisting of the spiritual powers of imagination (conceiving things); thought (reflecting upon realities); comprehension (understanding realities); and memory (remembering what we imagine, think, and understand). These are our inner powers, while sight, hearing, smell, taste, and feeling are our five outer powers, the agents of perception. The mind is the intermediary between the outer and inner powers, connecting them both.

In real life, our sight sees a flower, conveys this perception to the imagination, forming an image of the flower and transmitting this to our thought, which reflects upon it, grasps the flower's reality, and conveys this to comprehension, which delivers the image of it to our memory, which keeps it in its repository.

As we strive toward the perfections embedded within us to reach the spiritual capacity we are endowed with, how we utilize our power of choice and free will determines whether we develop the virtues of the soul—such as justice, equity, and goodness—and reach the heights of consciousness, or succumb to expressions of the material self—such as greed, tyranny, and injustice—and fall short of our capacity.

This is why a new chapter to the ongoing story of our evolving consciousness is needed. Our time seems to embody the characteristics of the biblical "time of the end." We need a renewal of the perennial truths that have gotten us this far.

Consciousness Changes with Experience

Our consciousness of who we are is further complicated by the multiple identities we carry with us all the time. Not only do many more identities exist now than ever before—ethnicity, nationality, language, religion, gender, socioeconomic class, age, sexual orientation, physical ability, education, occupation, and more—all of these interact in ways that impact all of the others.

These multiple identities converge, *and* are the cause of even more complex issues for us; they are all part of a system of privilege and oppression. Each of our multiple identities put us on either the privileged/dominant side of the identity continuum (whites, men, heterosexuals, Christians, etc.), or on the oppressed/subordinate side (any minority group we are a member of). This can make our awareness of who we are more confusing when we realize that some parts of who we identify as may be afforded certain privileges while other parts may be oppressed.

Ultimately, this tricks us into believing that these are our primary, maybe even only, identities, and that what is most important in determining who we are is dictated by these temporal aspects of ourselves.

The competing views of who we are create the need to defend or cling, which in turn creates pain and suffering if our identities are threatened. But they also create the conditions for growth and transformation, which ultimately lead to being able to embrace the one reality. So there is a purpose to our multiple identities, but they are not the end goal. They simply give us a basis for understanding how personal and social consciousness evolves.

Our multiple identities also create the illusion of multiple paths, multiple priorities, and multiple options to choose from in selecting our allegiance. But, as Chief Leon Shenandoah has put it, there is but one path, one identity, that has our true nature as its signpost:

Everything is laid out for you,
Your path is straight ahead of you.
Sometimes it's invisible but it's there,
You may not know where it's going,
But you have to follow that path.
It's the path to the Creator.
It's the only path there is.

Our consciousness is set up to allow us to see many things when there is really only one thing in front of us. Sometime after we are born our unified consciousness becomes divided. At some later point we become aware that we reside in a world built upon polarities, each one competing for our attention and allegiance. We continue to live within this world of dualities until we come to the further awareness that all the parts we have become so familiar with are actually components of a greater wholeness, within which we regain our consciousness of oneness.

Our understanding of reality gradually evolves as our consciousness evolves. Born with a limited consciousness, we transcend our own finite perspective over and over in our lives until we arrive at a glimpse of the infinite, which then becomes the wider base with which we understand everything else after that. Life is a process of moving from an underdeveloped, localized, fragmented consciousness toward a fully developed universal consciousness.

Once we have an experience of oneness and unity that is what we will want to strive to see everywhere. It is like looking above ground at a vast field of wells that appear from this perspective to be tapping independent sources of water, compared to being able to see from the underground perspective and knowing that there is really only one interconnected source of water. We realize our fullest potential as we transcend apparent barriers and limitations, eventually merging our individual consciousness with a boundless consciousness.

How we see ourselves, how we understand our personal identity, depends on our current level of consciousness. If we expand our consciousness enough to change our worldview, we are at the same time changing our identity, since we are really one with what we know. It is all interconnected; shifting our awareness shifts our level of consciousness, which shifts our sense of identity.

If the mind is silent, content, and focused on what does not change, we

> Where do you come from?
> *From the other world.*
> And where do you go?
> *Into the other world.*
> And what do you do in this world?
> *I jest with it by eating its bread and doing the works of the other world in it.*
> ~A conversation with
> Rabi'a of Basra

have gotten to our core identity, as well as to pure consciousness. As Peter Russell puts it, "The essential self is eternal; it never changes."

All the multiple identities we carry hide a single identity we all share. We all come from the same Creator, and will return to that Creator. Our eternal connection to the Creator is the essence of our fullest identity, of who we are at our unchanging core. If we think we are any of the multiple, hierarchical, dominant or subordinate identities that make up our temporal self, these are not who we are for eternity.

Eastern spiritual traditions say that identifying with—and desiring—the temporal is surely a cause of suffering. Attachment to the fleeting places hope on that which is not real, and does not last. Our choice to build up and maintain multiple identities creates tension and suffering within us and between others. To identify first and foremost with our eternal essence unites us with everyone.

If we could strip away all of our temporal identities, those aspects of ourselves that will disappear at death, what would remain? Our physical, genetic, social, and psychological identities are who we are, but only for the limited time we are on this earth. If we could take a more farsighted perspective, we might see that what remains after we continue our eternal journey from here is our eternal identity, our soul.

We are a merging of the temporary elements of earth and the lasting elements of heaven. Our threefold nature consists of body, mind, and soul. We are *physical beings*, with a body, a clear reflection of the world of creation; *human beings* with a mind, having a unique capacity for reflective consciousness, and, *spiritual beings* with a soul, a clear reflection of the Creator.

Although the soul is our divine reality, giving us our spiritual potential, it needs the mind, an intermediary between our physical and spiritual natures, to interact with in order to become one with the body. Who we become is a result of how these three natures interact with and influence each other.

Our true nature is that part of us that does not change, the unified whole we can become. As we integrate all of our multiple identities, including our eternal identity, we take on a unified identity that tells us who we are in both the temporal and eternal realms. As we identify equally with our eternal self and our temporal self, we become that eternal self.

The Search for Truth Expands Our Consciousness

I was recently moved by the story of a gospel singer who, not yet aware of her longing, was slowly but convincingly drawn to investigate life's deepest mysteries. This eventually became her conscious quest, and she was led to a new spiritual tradition that answered all of her unasked questions. She put the process she had embarked upon very succinctly: "If you have a question, go look for the answer; it will be there for you!"

We have but to set out on that open road before us, with eyes wide open, to seek answers to our deep questions. It will serve us well on this quest to dedicate some time, perhaps an hour a day, for reflection upon what we are finding along the way. There is a rich and deep spiritual heritage waiting to guide us into this adventure.

Jung points out an unexpected reward. "To find out what is truly individual in ourselves, profound reflection is needed; and suddenly we realize how uncommonly difficult the discovery of individuality in fact is." In other words, the power of our own consciousness, reflecting upon itself, reveals how connected we all are.

This is clearly seen in the great vision that came to Black Elk in his youth:

> *...I was standing on the highest mountain of them all, and round about beneath me was the whole hoop of the world. And while I stood there I saw more than I can tell and I understood more than I saw; for I was seeing in a sacred manner the shapes of all things in the spirit, and the shape of all shapes as they must live together like one being. And I saw that the sacred hoop of my people was one of many hoops that made one circle, and in the center grew one mighty flowering tree to shelter all the children of one mother and one father. And I saw that it was holy.*

Consciousness is a gift designed to help us see beyond what is evident, delve into the hidden meanings of the obvious, and extract the essence of what we are pondering. The deepest meaning available to us becomes apparent with meditation, which allows us to transcend the purely physical, enter the realm of the spirit, and discover the reality of things. Through conscious reflection, we gain second sight, our "power of insight," or illumination.

We cannot search for truth to live by without conscious effort. If we are satisfied with what has been handed down to us, we will remain complacent, probably even inert. If we continually seek the unknown and make it known, new knowledge, especially lasting and meaningful, will guide our way to the perennial truth of oneness.

This search for truth is a key principle of a timeless wisdom that recognizes the individual soul as a reflection of divine Reality. Once the life of the spirit, or the quest of the soul, has begun, it is never without fulfillment. Spiritual discernment, development, and search always bring us closer to the Creator.

The world's religions agree upon this. Every sacred tradition expresses some form of the familiar "Seek and ye shall find." From Judaism, "If from thence thou shalt seek the Lord thy God, thou shalt find him...;" or, as in Islam, "He who approaches near to Me one span, I will approach near to him one cubit… and whoever approaches Me walking, I will come to him running."

Shankara's Hindu/Buddhist Vedanta perspective also makes the individual effort required very evident: "The nature of the one Reality must be known by one's own clear spiritual perception; it cannot be known through a pundit (learned man). Similarly, the form of the moon can only be known through one's own eyes. How can it be known through others?"

In our time, the investigation of reality has been made a primary spiritual principle by Baha'u'llah. This involves discovering truth for ourselves, not following blindly, but seeing with our own eyes, hearing with our own ears, and utilizing the power of our own mind. If we use the power of our own spirit, an emanation of the Divine spirit, and if we "investigate the religions to discover the principles underlying their foundations we will find they agree, for the fundamental reality of them is one and not multiple…All the prophets have been the promoters of these principles."

In this age, the right of every one of us to investigate reality for ourselves is the most fundamental of all human rights; exercising this right can bring us the greatest of benefits, not only in this life but in the life to come. That human consciousness is endowed with the intellectual, moral, spiritual, and aesthetic capacities needed to undertake such an effort is evidence enough that this right exists. Our own spiritual development depends on this to transcend earlier levels of consciousness.

Our inherent urge to understand reality expands and fulfills our consciousness, enabling us to acquire the wisdom available to us as co-creators of this creation. An expanded consciousness is a means for advancing civilization. Those who seek truth facilitate their own transformation as well as the transformation of society.

Ervin Laszlo says our challenge is "reorienting our vision." We need a good compass to guide us that can set standards and direct our steps. These ideals, he says, are found in our existing cultural and spiritual heritage, and "still have a latent power to motivate actions and influence decisions:"

> "The great ideals of the world religions...embody perennial values...and should be reaffirmed... There is, for example, the Christian vision of universal brotherhood governed by man's love for a God of all men and for his fellow human beings. There is Judaism's historical vision of an elected people in whom all the families of the earth are to be blessed. Islam has a universal vision of an ultimate community of God, man, nature, and society. The essential goal of the Baha'i Faith is to achieve a vision that is world embracing and could lead to the unity of mankind and the establishment of a world civilization based on peace and justice. Hinduism envisions matter as but the outward manifestation of spirit and urges attunement to cosmic harmony through the varied paths of yoga. Buddhism, too, perceives all reality as interdependent, and teaches man to achieve union with it through rejection of the drives and desires of a separate ego. Confucianism finds supreme harmony in disciplined and ordered human relationships, and Taoism finds such harmony in nature and naturalness. The African tribal religions conceive of a great community of the living and the dead, to which each

person belongs unless he willfully creates imbalances between the seen and unseen forces in and around himself."

These are the perennial ideals based on universal human values. In their original and purest form, they can guide our steps into a sustainable future. In our search for truth, with our consciousness expanded, we come to a remarkable realization. We find that what we thought was out there is also within us. We find that essence of ourselves that unites us with all creation, all beings, and divinity itself. As Deepak Chopra has said, "What you seek, you already are."

> Everything that is in the heavens, on earth,
> and under the earth
> is penetrated with connectedness,
> penetrated with relatedness.
> ~Hildegard of Bingen

Our consciousness has its source in unity. And this is where our search leads us; the goal of the spiritual journey is the transpersonal reality of the boundless consciousness that unites us with all of creation, with divine reality.

Our quest is one of remembering where we came from, what our purpose here is, and where we are going. As our consciousness grows, all the pairs of opposites we encounter matter less and less. We gradually find a comfort level with them and eventually they even seem to merge into a greater whole.

At the deepest level, all things are one. As Brother Wayne Teasdale said, "Every person is a mystic. The call to the spiritual journey is always inviting us. We need only respond. In this summons, in the cave of the heart, we are all one."

While each spiritual and religious tradition includes detailed beliefs and practices that promote the spiritual life, it is only in the mystical branches of those traditions that a deeper path to oneness is laid out. The mystic path is meant to lead us to union with the source of our being. Teasdale implies that we don't have to be part of any one those traditions to have this same deep desire, or urge. It is an all-human trait, or characteristic, to want to seek union with the deepest part of who we are that comes from and connects us to our Creator, or to all of creation.

It is on this so-called 'mystical' path that everyone will find the same thing – at the deepest level all things are connected in an undeniable oneness. And all sacred traditions have their own tools and practices that are specifically designed to help any of us get there – prayer, meditation, deepening in the sacred writings, remembrance (of God), whirling dance, upholding the highest of ethical standards, ritual, initiation, vision quest, pilgrimage, yoga, seeing with the inner eye (the eye of oneness), and service to others, just to name a few.

Principle 2

Love is the underlying force of evolution

Even with flux, the direction of evolution's arrow has been toward greater complexity, resulting in wider circles of collective unity. This flow has given life a trajectory that eventually creates order out of chaos, and builds complex systems of cooperation and harmony out of simple and random interactions. Supporting this eternal process is the organic, organizing force of love.

Never have the effects of love's force been more apparent, or important. Daily circumstances bring to light spontaneous expressions of empathy, altruistic care, compassion, reconciliation, and service to humanity. Love, in all its forms and disguises, still flourishes in a world wounded by hatred. Through it all, ignorance and knowledge, doubt and certitude, disbelief and faith, we know we will endure in this journey aided by the ever-present force of love.

As we consciously integrate this divine force into our own lives, we feel the inherent unifying force of love meant to evolve personal and collective potential to its highest level possible. In this sacred space, we love all things with a pure heart, knowing love will conquer all forms of hate, for this is the straight path of evolution.

2

Attraction Alters the Course of Civilizations

Without contraries is no progression.
Attraction and repulsion, reason and energy, love and hate,
are necessary to human existence.

-William Blake

All because of love when it arrived my temporal life
from then on changed to eternal.

-Rumi

As our spiritual life takes hold, we become dissolved in the fire of love. Ecstasy, once tasted, gives way to enthusiasm and longing, which propel us onward toward the goal of our desire. The spiritual life represents an awakening of love, fervor in the soul, as we glimpse traces of eternal truth and oneness within the entire range of diverse phenomena in the physical universe. This is accompanied by relinquishing self-love in order to become united with the beloved.

Rumi tells us, "All because of love," our temporal life is changed to eternal. As we learn about life and death, we may begin to wonder if this is all there is. A little further on, we may also grow weary of the confusion and conflicts of this life. Is Rumi referring to love with a capital L, what we can think of as divine love?

Altruistic Love Changes Everything

The temporal world is where separation, duality, and conflict-based perspectives reign. Yet, when we shift our perspective from the temporal to the eternal realm, we enter a mindful state of awareness that enables us to experience a realm of changelessness, as past, present, and future become one continuous moment. From this vantage point, of the eternal self, emotions such as happiness or love can become lasting. In the temporal world, they are often fleeting.

Of the three forms of happiness, "physical happiness" (which results from the sensory pleasures of the body, such as good food, delightful sounds, or beautiful sights), "social happiness" (which derives from human interactions that warm the heart and generate

> *The soul enamoured of My Truth never ceases to serve the whole world in general.*
> ~St. Catherine of Siena

feelings or emotions of giving or receiving affection), and "spiritual happiness," it is only the third form that offers a deeper, fuller, pervasive, underlying joy that can be ever-present.

Spiritual joy is more of a constant calmness, a perpetual state of acceptance of the way things are and the way things happen, like the deep ocean which remains still though there may be stormy waves above it. The lasting happiness and love of the eternal self comes about through a change of heart, one that allows us to transcend the temporal elements of life, and the conflicts that can pull us in to a frenzied state of being. This is what leads us to the kind of love Rumi is talking about.

Altruistic love comes from the divine self, being inspired by a love of the eternal. As the divine self steps outside of the temporal realm, gets a perspective of the whole, and recognizes who we are at our essence, it comes to understand that the source of lasting happiness is our awareness of our own divinity. This is what allows us to live within a perpetual state of love. As Mother Teresa has said, "We have been created in order to love and to be loved."

Referred to as the mother emotion, though nearly impossible to define, love is the most powerful attractive force in the universe. Love is the power that binds together all the various elements of the material world. Love is the magnetic force that directs the movement of the planets in the heavenly realms.

On the human and social level, love is attraction to the qualities and attributes of other human beings. On a spiritual level, love is the selfless attraction to others and our Creator. Spiritual love generates the lasting emotion of spiritual happiness, as this is what establishes our connection with our Beloved, and creates a form of unity with the love object that brings a steady state of joyfulness. When Rumi experienced this force in his life, he was transformed; his temporal life became his eternal life.

Our choice is to live in separation from all things or in union with all things. The eternal self, guided by the most powerful force in the universe – love – seeks integration, wholeness, and communion with the soul, others, and the Creator. Its perspective is a seamless, unified worldview consisting of one reality. It knows that its life is part of every other life, and therefore in harmony with creation.

The Love Ethic

If we are like islands in the sea, appearing to the eye as separate but really connected on a deeper level, as William James suggested, wouldn't we, collectively, not only come to this conscious realization eventually but also begin to shift our thinking to accommodate this reality in our everyday lives and actions?

And if we were so deeply connected, wouldn't it also seem that we would begin to recognize that we *are* made for transcending the illusion of separation, caring for whom we are connected to, and knowing that our true security lies in the good of the whole? In other words, in this holistic consciousness, wouldn't our greatest act in this world be to express love, compassion, caring, and charity, in all things we do?

Understanding the path of our own evolution means awakening to our own humanity, to that specialness that is ours only. And what is that specialness other than having been designed to live according to the law of compassion? From Paul's letter to the Corinthians (1, 13.8) to Kierkegaard to D.H. Lawrence to M.L. King, Jr. to Cornel West, we are often reminded that we are inwardly guided by the love ethic.

Could universal, unconditional love be *The Creator's Gift* that was hidden within each and every person, as in the traditional indigenous story?

Once upon a time, a long time ago, the Creator called a meeting of all the people of creation, except the human people. When everyone else arrived, He said, "I have a special gift for the human people, but they are not ready for it yet. Where should I put it so that they will not be able to find it, until they are ready for it?"

The Salmon people spoke first, and said, "If you give the gift to us, we will take it down to the bottom of the ocean where no human being will ever find it."

The Creator said, "Thank you for your offer, but the gift will not be safe there because one day the human beings will build special machines to take them there."

The great Buffalo people who roamed the vast prairies said, "We will bury it deep in the middle of the grasslands; there is nothing there to interest the humans."

The Creator said, "One day the humans will build cities and connect every part of the plains and grasslands with roads and railways and nothing will stay hidden."

Then the Eagle people said, "We will take it to the moon."

Once again the Creator, in his infinite wisdom, said, "They will go there, too."

These clever suggestions went on for most of the day, and each time the Creator gave His thanks to all the people of creation, but explained that in their endless curiosity to explore every part of the world the humans would find it.

After a long silence, Grandmother Mole, the shyest of all, tugged at the Creator's clothing. He bent down, and she whispered into His ear.

Then the Creator smiled with delight, and all the Animal people felt His warmth. The Creator said, "That is the answer. We will put the gift for the humans within their own hearts. They will never think to look there!" And that is what they did.

Rather than let its purpose remain unfulfilled, our challenge is to be conscious of this precious gift, bring it out, and pass it on to others.

Science now tells us that we have been hardwired to connect, cooperate, *and* to be empathic. Our Creator has embedded within us multiple gifts, or capacities, to achieve our potential in becoming the spiritual beings we already are. All we have to do is bring to the surface what has been buried within us to fulfill our potential.

When these potentialities do not come forth, crises occur. While studying the rising rates of mental problems and emotional distress among U.S. children and adolescents, an eminent group of children's doctors, research scientists, and mental health professionals found a lack of connectedness to other people – and to moral and spiritual meaning – to be at the heart of the problem.

This same group presented scientific evidence from the field of neuroscience that human beings are "hardwired to connect." They said our brains need connections to other people and to moral meaning for "essential health and human flourishing." This is one of the first efforts to utilize "hard science" in recommending that our society pay attention to young people's moral, spiritual, and religious needs.

Ironically, it is not always the natural law of Survival of the Fittest that prevails. In fact, its opposite, the natural law of cooperation, is what enables transcendence from self to society to succeed. As explored further in chapter seven, Darwin's natural law does not negate but rather complements this natural need to cooperate, which is actually called the Golden Rule by the world's religions, and holds strong through all the kingdoms of life, animal and human equally. The natural law of cooperation implies that "the rationality of the universe" has an underlying purpose or direction to it, as Einstein surmised.

Extending our innate need to connect, and to cooperate, to its next logical level, Jeremy Rifkin, in *The Empathic Civilization*, says at our deepest nature we are "homo empathicus." He reports that "empathy neurons" have been discovered that allow us to feel and experience another's situation as if it were our own. Hardwired to be empathic, this innate consciousness has been steadily evolving over our history. Rifkin wants us to consider this question: is the Age of Aquarius really the Age of Empathy?

No longer is it out of place to wonder if we are all born with these capacities, and that it just takes time or the right circumstances for them to emerge. It is not a stretch to ask if all the related virtues, like love, compassion, caring, charity, mercy, service, sacrifice, helpfulness, cooperation, courtesy, kindness, and thoughtfulness, are also hardwired into who we are as spiritual human beings.

We seem to know intuitively that caring for and assisting others in time of need without concern for our own needs not only feels right but also contributes to our own sense of well-being and happiness. Altruism is love, compassion, and kindness in action. What we are witnessing more of recently is that certain tragedies in the world set off a compassion trigger in the brain and we feel called to action. We saw this in the overwhelming response to the 2004 Indian Ocean tsunami that took over 200,000 lives. Charitable donations to an independent UN relief fund immediately following this totaled $6.25 billion, unlike any response ever seen before.

There have always been exceptions to this pattern of expanding circles of compassion, but they are also part of the pattern, seen as shadow behaviors of old, deeply engrained ways rearing their head in resistance to progress. A stark example of this is seen in fearful and hateful responses to immigrants and refugees. While relocation has always been central to the human condition, recent anti-immigration tendencies, such as a desire to close borders to those displaced by war and persecution, represent part of the clash of opposing forces needed to bring about complete transformation (explained further in chapter four) and the final death-throes of an ill-fated system based on prejudice, greed, and fear, which is being replaced by an inclusive system rooted in love and altruism.

The overriding rule of natural selection and evolution is still seen to be "generalized reciprocity," or "reciprocal altruism." Evolutionary psychologists believe that various impulses designed for the "practical purpose of bringing beneficial exchange" (such as: generosity, gratitude, and empathy for those who reciprocate) are built into us. These are found in all cultures, they say.

Jung's notion of archetypes is further evidence of our being hardwired for altruistic love. The psyche of a newborn child is not a *"tabula rasa* in the sense that there is absolutely nothing in it." The child's brain "is predetermined by heredity," and expresses "inherited instincts and preformed patterns... They are the archetypes, which...produce...astonishing mythological parallels," and are, therefore, "inherited possibilities of ideas" that represent "the authentic element of spirit," or "a spiritual goal toward which the whole nature of man strives." The archetype is that which potentially connects us to our own divine nature.

The Force of Attraction Writ Large

From a distance, we can see a direction to both biological evolution and human history. Neither is a smooth, strictly linear process. But with perspective, we see a process of how love (and the lack of it) can change individuals, groups, communities, nations, and even civilization as a whole.

Human history has its ups and downs, and agendas at odds with each other. Cycles of conquest and expansion, fragmentation and collapse, have characterized the rise and fall of civilizations forever. As civilizations come and go, civilization itself continues to flourish, growing in scope and complexity. Progress is made; new forms of disruption come along, yet new and more complex forms of cooperation also arise.

To sustain this innate pattern for a harmonious future, an inclusive altruistic love in its fullest is needed, now more than ever. Our challenge is to become more aware of our inner spiritual nature, and let this direct our entire lives.

We are our spiritual essence. Directing our aspirations toward the heights of our spiritual potential will infuse altruistic love into a burdened world. If we had as our deepest ambition to help bring about the achievement on earth of such a spiritual civilization, we would, according to Baha'u'llah:

> "Be generous in prosperity, and thankful in adversity. Be worthy of the trust of thy neighbor...a treasure to the poor, an admonisher to the rich, an answerer of the cry of the needy...fair in thy judgment, and guarded in thy speech. Be unjust to no man, and show meekness to all men. Be as a lamp unto them that walk in darkness, a joy to the sorrowful...a haven for the distressed, an upholder and defender of the victim of oppression...a breath of life to the body of mankind."

All of these spiritual qualities, attributes, and virtues are offspring of the mother of all emotions: love. When these virtues are put into action on the collective level, we will see even more clearly how attraction alters civilizations.

Of the four forces of nature identified by physics (gravity, the strong nuclear force, the weak nuclear force, and the electro-magnetic force), it is not surprising that attractive forces appear overall stronger than repulsive forces. Nor is it surprising that seeking a theory of everything that would unify these four fundamental forces of nature has now become the Holy Grail of modern physics.

Love, as the most powerful attractive force in the entire universe, is further seen as the primary principle of a divine order. It was Empedocles, in ancient Greece, who suggested that the four primal elements—earth, air, fire, and water—are at the whim of the two opposing cosmic forces, Love and Strife. The attracting force of Love or the averting force of Strife dictates all change in the universe. He proposed alternating cosmic cycles of Love (or harmony) and Strife (or discord), in which unity and multiplicity alternate in cycles.

These alternating cycles operate in the affairs of humanity, as well. At times a natural balance may occur between the two forces; at other times it seems a true struggle ensues between them. A significant difference, however, is that in the cycle involving the primal elements it is the law of *balance* that is primary, while in the cycle involving our own collective evolution it is the law of *perpetual progress* that is primary, with love ultimately winning out over discord.

In the cycles of human evolution, altruistic love has become the standard, progressing over the centuries from a feeling of emotional warmth toward others to the practice of unconditional love directed toward seemingly unconnected others. It is an attractive force operating according to certain timeless laws and principles, which we become more aware of and subject to as time moves on.

This transformational process is seen in the history of religions as well.

When Jesus of Nazareth, recognized by his followers as "The Christ," went beyond earlier understanding and made the heart of his teachings "love your enemies, bless them that curse you, do good to them that hate you" (Matthew 5:44), he not only expanded the consciousness of his followers, but in responding courageously to this new moral standard by putting it into action, the early believers endured three centuries of persecution and martyrdom, all for the sake of experiencing authentic relationships. Such is the attractive power of altruistic love.

Because we live in a time of social unrest, economic imbalance, political upheaval, and environmental crises, we must seriously consider the collective implication to this force of attraction. If what we collectively think is what we get back, then thinking positively and acting accordingly with our collective will would bring into existence an altruistic-based civilization; this is the power of attraction writ large.

We've been gradually moving toward this goal since our beginning moments on Earth. Spiritual quests and religious practice, in their purest form, are intended to be the cause of unity and love, a remedy to social ills and shortcomings.

That altruistic love can bring about a spiritual civilization is at the heart of the Buddhist practice of *metta*. This state of mind, achieved through a specific meditation called metta bhavana or loving-kindness meditation, extends universal love and goodwill to all beings by putting into action the strong wish for the welfare and happiness of others. In a wakeful meditative state, metta practitioners focus on the following four phrases: May I be happy; May I be well; May I be safe; May I be peaceful and at ease. Then they shift the focus to another person or group: May you be happy; May you be well; May you be safe; May you be peaceful and at ease. Then they expand their emphasis to a universal plane: May all beings be happy; May all beings be well; May all beings be safe; May all beings be peaceful and at ease. This altruistic attitude of love and friendliness develops a mind of accommodativeness and benevolence, seeks the well-being and happiness of others, and mirrors the unconditional love of a mother for her child, yet on a universal scale.

When the supreme gift of love is all embracing, there is a mutual recognition that places our common divinity above all else. This sincere, unselfish love allows for a deeper, more respectful and more honoring relationship that creates a ripple effect touching everything around it. The method for achieving this degree of love is to see all of creation through the eyes of the One who created it all.

Seeing through our own eyes, we tend to see distinctions, separations, and imperfections first. But looking through the eyes of the Creator, we see the whole first, the spiritual reality of the holiness and oneness that is always right before our eyes.

This vision of oneness is what the force of love is leading us toward. The principle of altruistic love is built upon having—and acting according to—the knowledge of this oneness of all creation.

Active altruistic love, acceptance of the other without judgment or conditions, characterizes the highest levels of moral development. While selfish interests take over in the lower stages, as moral values become increasingly universalized we reach our fullest potential, and spiritual values win out.

If this innate capacity for altruism had not saved us from our own destruction in our earliest history as a human community, how much more has this been the case over the course of our long and troublesome recent history? Social aggression and conflicts, though at times characteristic of our social, economic, political, and even religious systems, are not representations of our true nature. They are, rather, distortions of the human spirit.

Humanity evolves, just as individuals do, through stages. From childlike innocence and vulnerability to grasping on to a preference for conflict and injustice, we are entering a time of more focused integration of our newfound abilities, while also acknowledging our growing responsibilities. We are currently approaching the end of humanity's adolescent stage of moral development and its transition to maturity. With this comes an accompanying shift of emphasis from power seeking to pursuing moral and socially productive ends.

Love Eliminates All Forms of Prejudice

With the expansion of consciousness comes the raising of standards. We know now that an appropriate response for our time that will break long

30

entrenched habits and patterns of hatred is simply replacing that with love. We have seen this trend in the progress of the human spirit, most visibly in the rise of humanitarianism.

The evolution of virtue has slowly advanced, transforming the killing of a rival from a noble deed to a shameful murder, while making the distinction between good and evil ever sharper. Since the founding of the Royal Humane Society in England in 1774, there has been a growing feeling that the world is changing for the better.

A rising tide of humanitarianism followed this and signaled a new goal in the consciousness of humanity: caring for and giving altruistically to any and all members of humanity in need. This trend toward compassion and justice expanded during the 19th century with the founding of the profession of nursing, the outlawing of slavery worldwide, and the founding of the Red Cross and the Salvation Army.

A closer look at this rising tide reveals a long, protracted process of altruistic love unfolding, though fraught with tremendous struggle. Starting seriously in the 1850s in the U.S., we have the Abolitionist Movement, the Emancipation Proclamation (1862), followed by the 13th, 14th, and 15th Amendments and the Civil Rights Acts of 1866, 1871, and 1875, representing a complete transformation of the U.S. and its Constitution, at least in matters of a humanitarian nature.

Though another 100 years passed before the Civil Rights Movement of the 1950-60s, and the struggle still lives on today, the evolution of consciousness is undeniable, as it continues to deliberately unfold across time, while deeply rooted prejudices and the systems they give rise to slowly but surely lose their hold.

The force of love writ large—as well as the evolution of consciousness— is recognized further through our understanding of how the concept of the human race itself has evolved. Race did not come into play in ancient societies. The Greeks were in some ways more "equal opportunity" societies than most today. They created distinctions based only on religion, social status or class, and in some cases language.

Appearing in the English language relatively recently, only 500 years ago, race was first used as a term to separate us. It was thought that there were many "races," which contributed to privileges for some and disadvantages for others. The result, racism, is still one of the most challenging social issues of our time.

Yet now, research in genetics, genealogy, and molecular anthropology gives us much more to consider. The discovery of DNA is a paradigm-shifter; we now understand that scientific truth is relative and continuously unfolding.

What science once had no way of knowing can now be understood from DNA: all human beings alive today are the descendants of ancestors who set out from central Africa some 70,000 years ago on a long migration that spanned the earth.

As the children of our primeval parents spread out and moved into different continents of the globe, it was environment, or geography, that caused genetic variation and differences in skin tone, not biology. What DNA tells us completely shatters our previous worldview. We are no longer just the ethnic or national heritage we thought we were; we are all members of the "tribe of nomads—at home nowhere and ceaselessly on the way to someplace else."

We are world wanderers, global migrants; this is what is written in our genes. The recent increase in numbers of immigrants and refugees worldwide, although massive, is not new. Throughout history there have always been forces that have pushed or pulled peoples from their place of origin.

But this new information from our DNA changes how we see our connection to each other, and what we think of as home. We can all now begin to understand the Earth as our common homeland; we are all global villagers, put in this unique setting to specifically but gradually and inevitably recognize our oneness in all our diversity.

Most important from our new understanding of DNA is the interrelatedness of all human beings; we all share the same common ancestors. Even with over 7 billion of us today, measuring our surprisingly close relation to each other, we find that no human being—of any so-called "race"—can be less closely related to any other human being than approximately 50th cousin; most of us are a lot closer than that.

Before we can trace back our ancestry 50 generations, every family tree, of whatever origin, meets and merges into one genetic tree of all humanity. As we integrate these new understandings, our worldview is gradually shifting, too.

The idea that there are human "races" is an illusion. There is only one human race, and we are among the most genetically similar of all species. The obvious surface-level differences we observe are literally only skin deep. 85% of all human variation exists within, not between, "races" or any local population.

Race is a biological fiction; yet it is a social fact with very real social consequences. Race as a plurality, and a social construction, was learned; we can unlearn this and replace it with the reality that race, too, is a unified whole.

With the help of science, and especially the relatively recent discovery of DNA, our consciousness has expanded and shifted once again. Today, we understand that a concept that once separated us, "race" no longer needs to keep us apart.

At a moment when it appeared otherwise, in the wake of widespread racially-charged violence around the country, at a memorial service in Dallas for five slain police officers, President Barack Obama assured Americans that, "Although…we wonder if the divides of race in America can ever be bridged…I'm here to insist that we're not as divided as we seem…I know we'll make it because of what I've experienced in my own life…" As this nation's first African American president, his optimistic view of race relations in America gives us reason to believe that the false constructs promulgated by incomplete notions of race will be dismantled and replaced by true civil rights and lasting social justice.

Our understanding of the biological truth of our unity as a human race has evolved in the 20th and 21st century. The human spirit has evolved through the Women's Rights Movement, the League of Nations, the United Nations and its Universal Declaration of Human Rights, the Civil Rights Movement, and many other human rights initiatives creating a growing commitment to these altruistic concerns.

In the past decade alone, each natural disaster has seen a greater outpouring of compassion, altruism, and humanitarian aid, from New Orleans to New Zealand to Haiti and Japan. Once again, at a press conference immediately following the 2011 earthquake in Japan, President Obama noted, "For all our differences in culture or language or religion, ultimately, humanity is one."

This is the essence of our transformation of consciousness. Knowing that we are one human family creates a consciousness of selfless, altruistic caring for all other members of our family. As love—the most powerful of all forces—continues to gain momentum, we will see the rise of a spiritual civilization. All the prophets have come to support this strongest of universal forces, and to teach the principles of a morality upon which an inclusive and compassionate civilization can be built.

Our expansion of consciousness has led us to wider and wider expressions of altruistic love. With this as our modus operandi, conflict, disunity, or estrangement between people would simply not be possible, just as the force of gravity between two bodies could never push them apart. Both are entirely and always an attractive force.

Prejudice is a manifestation of love's opposite force. When love prevails, any form of its opposite will be stifled. Love's celebration in story, myth, and poetry across time and place has been greater than any of the other human capacities. Love's supremacy means it is in the unique and powerful position of bringing about the realization of oneness in those who truly understand its meaning and purpose.

Whether a soldier on a battlefield protects another, or black and white march together for civil rights, their common commitment creates a deep bond of unity. Altruistic love that emerges in groups, especially under duress, transforms communities, cultures, and ultimately the world.

Love is the safeguard for human diversity. The realization of the oneness of the human race eliminates the notion that any one group is in some way superior to the rest of humanity. Any assertion of superiority is without foundation. Prejudice is a baneful heritage, due only to a limited consciousness, and will surely be replaced by the stronger force of love.

Too much of our history has been shaped by the disease of racism. Human dignity has been compromised and our evolution has been slowed by its influence, yet deliberate and sustained effort will overcome its devastating effects. As Chief Joseph has noted, "Much trouble and blood would be saved if we opened our hearts more." Only "genuine love, extreme patience, true humility and prayerful reflection will succeed" in eliminating racial bias in human affairs. "Close your eyes to racial differences," is Baha'u'llah's counsel, "and welcome all with the light of oneness."

Recognition that humanity is a single people with a common destiny will cause a shift in society as a whole, resulting in a reorganization of all life, by giving practical expression to the primary principle of equality for all its members regardless of color, greed, or gender. This will enable all individuals to realize their inherent potential and thus contribute to an ever-advancing civilization.

This is a view that many scientists can understand and accept, as well. "Give evolution long enough," Robert Wright says, "and reciprocal altruism will arise yet again—and again and again and again..." on ever greater levels each time.

Love is a transformative power. Mystics and saints have long known that Love is the highest truth, that the universe comes from Love, and that the universe is sustained by Love. Love is the primary expression of Creation. The power of Love unveils the illusion of the physical world and takes us beyond birth and death to the world of spiritual wonderment. Teilhard de Chardin put it this way, "Love is the...affinity which links and draws together the elements of the world...Love, in fact, is the expression and agent of universal synthesis."

Abdu'l-Baha, son of Baha'u'llah, captures the meaning of love as the underlying force of evolution that will ultimately overtake and dissolve all forms of prejudice: Love is the "living link" that unites "God with humanity," that assures "the progress of every illumined soul." Love is the greatest law ruling our time, the "unique power" that binds together the diverse "elements of this material world, the supreme magnetic force" that directs "the movements of the spheres in the celestial realms."

Love reveals "with unfailing and limitless power the mysteries latent in the universe. Love is the spirit of life unto the adorned body of mankind, the establisher of true civilization in this mortal world..."

Principle 3

Justice maintains the inherent balance of life

Justice is the embodiment of divine order on earth. It is a supreme force for moral rightness, social equality and harmony, and a central principle in all the world's spiritual traditions. Among the conditions of a spiritually-based social order is a system of reward and punishment, the twin pillars of justice, which teach humanity to know the difference between right and wrong and to act accordingly.

Since antiquity, justice has balanced the scales of truth and fairness, as the cornerstone for the protection of human rights. Equitable and just relationships have evolved as human social interactions have become more complex. In our time, justice is the one means capable of harnessing the potentialities of globalization for the betterment and advancement of civilization. The fate of humanity in the 21st century depends upon the further unfolding of the two principles of unity and justice to bring about awareness of divine unity in the world of creation.

The challenge for achieving justice in our time is to turn toward oneness, realize the consciousness of the oneness of humanity, and allow justice to become the force for unity it is intended to be. A global system of unitive justice is the purest reflection of absolute unity possible on this earth.

3

Culture and the Evolution of Justice

Injustice anywhere is a threat to justice everywhere.
                                        -Martin Luther King, Jr.

*More souls are crammed onto this planet than ever, and there is the real
prospect of commensurably great peril. At the same time there is the prospect
of building the infrastructure for a planetary first: enduring global concord…
which is to say: winning will depend on not wanting other peoples to lose.*
                                        -Robert Wright

From a distance, we can see that there has been a progressive evolution of justice throughout the history of civilization. Before any codification of laws, in relatively homogenous communities, oral tradition sufficed. As communities grew, expanded, and interacted, greater measures were needed to separate right from wrong. With each passing millennium, there has been a greater certainty about what to do with acts of injustice. The arrow of time has carried with it the means to build ever more equitable social contracts; we now have a need for a global justice system.

With the greatest advancements of material civilization having come at the expense of spiritual qualities and attributes, it is clear that only a balanced approach benefits both the material and the spiritual aspects of civilization.

These twin aspects, like wings of a bird, are both essential for ensuring true progress.

The key to balanced progress is moderation. When civilization is balanced, and progresses on all fronts moderately, society flourishes, and becomes a source of goodness and opportunity for all. True justice is only achievable when the evolution of society is balanced, drawing equally from material and spiritual resources.

Culture as a Medium for Growth

Culture is like an organism that grows from a simple state to a complex system. Culture is so basic to human life, so all-pervasive, that, on the one hand, it is overlooked or taken for granted, while on the other hand, it can represent all of what we think we need to know to become fully worthwhile human beings.

Culture determines the ways that people everywhere respond to, share, organize, interpret, and pass on life's challenges. Far from being static, culture is ever changing. Culture, with its myriad ways of challenging and stretching our thinking, is a primary catalyst to the evolution of consciousness, which in turn contributes to the advancement and expansion of social justice.

From the Latin, *cultura*, culture means to care for, to cultivate, or to help grow. Culture as a medium for growth has its clearest parallel in biology. Bacteria and other microorganisms are grown in a laboratory in an appropriate "culture," a specially prepared nourishing substance designed to foster growth.

Humanity is also divided into separate cultures, with each person being the product of the culture in which he or she lives. Culture is the primary catalyst for both individual and collective growth, essential to both the evolution of consciousness and justice. As in biology, human culture is the laboratory writ large within which we grow.

Though differences exist between the cultures of the world, to place one above or below any of the others for any reason would create an open door to prejudice, racism, and genocide. As Maori elder Rose Pere has said, "No culture is more or less important than another—to suggest that there is, is to criticize the Creator."

> *O love, thy bonds are so sweet and so strong that they bind angels and saints together...*
> *In this union there is no difference between rich and poor, between nation and nation;*
> *all contradiction is excluded, for by this love crooked things are made straight and difficulties reconciled.*
>
> ~St. Catherine of Genoa

Some say cultural growth is random, others that it is directional. But this is not a simple "either/or" matter. Our collective evolution contains elements of both randomness and purposeful direction, though purpose appears to be winning out.

In the long run, it's looking like our collective journey has brought us to the threshold of our long-awaited collective coming of age. Seeming signs of randomness, such as prejudice, exploitation, and wars, have marked our immature stages, but can inspire us to more seriously take on the responsibilities of collective maturity.

Ken Wilber's Integral Theory identifies a direction to culture, with stages of growth each having their own qualities. *Traditional* culture, with a mythic-literal religious orientation, sees belief in the Bible as literally true, and holds nationalistic, ethnocentric, and patriarchal views. *Modern* culture, with a rational or scientific orientation, sees universal, scientific truths as more evident. *Postmodern* culture maintains a plurality of worldviews. But is this the highest level of cultural evolution?

Robert Wright says that our evolution has taken a directional process of weaving people into larger and richer webs of interdependence over the course of centuries. "The more closely we examine...the drift of human history, the more there seems to be a point to it all," a "core pattern" that captures history's basic trajectory. New technologies have encouraged new forms of win-win interactions, creating repeating patterns of expanding growth in evolution and social complexity.

Wright concludes, "Globalization, it seems to me, has been in the cards not just since the invention of the telegraph or the steamship, or even the written word or the wheel, but since the invention of life. The current age... is the natural outgrowth of several billion years of unfolding non-zero-sum logic."

This is one instance where a scientific perspective cannot be separated from a spiritual one. Wright's conclusion has its parallel, from the history of religion, in this statement of Baha'u'llah's, written in the middle of the nineteenth century: "All men have been created to carry forward an ever-advancing civilization." Accordingly, as we will soon see, culture grows and evolves toward wholeness and unity.

Cultural Evolution in Historical Perspective

Earlier in history, when cultural groups were isolated from one another, they were better able to maintain their own traditions, beliefs, and values. Though there were some internal struggles, tribal and indigenous cultural groups typically had fewer sources of external conflict to contend with; they maintained their own way of life.

Traditional communities were intentionally designed to sustain community traditions. The coming together of the entire community for rites, ceremonies, and storytelling served to reaffirm the spiritual wellbeing of the community.

Later, as cultures moved around, expanded into others' territory, and became imperialistic, their beliefs, values, and worldviews came into conflict, and struggle became the norm. New cultures emerged when two or more mixed. This is where the two primary forces of evolution—*conservatism* and *dynamism*—also came into play.

The dynamic force of change challenged tradition, or the status quo, even more. Thus, the twin opposing forces of tradition/conservatism vs. change/dynamism can be seen as laws governing the process of cultural growth and development.

Conservatism is the force that contributes to the retention of information, beliefs, customs, and other aspects of culture, and to maintaining them and passing them on to the next generation. Dynamism comprises all those elements that function to change the contents, meanings, and forms of culture over time. These two opposing forces can be envisioned as opposite ends of a spectrum.

Throughout history, interaction between the forces of conservatism and dynamism has been a fact of life, threatening traditional ways of life with exploitation, oppression, and domination, which has led to increased chaos and conflict.

This inherent struggle has gradually taken the form of a battle between sacred and secular values, as in the recent "Jihad vs. McWorld" phenomenon, the latest expression of a conflict always characterizing the end of one phase of cultural evolution and the beginning of another. This is also understood as the "death pangs" of an old order merging with the "birth pangs" of a new advance in society.

The Pattern of Collective Evolution

The entire history of cultural evolution can be seen, from a distance, as a process consisting of three essential steps: moving from unity to plurality and, at some point in the future, back to unity. This can also be expressed as *oneness* followed by *duality* followed by *oneness*.

First, the earliest indigenous communities were inherently unified by virtue of their common traditions, beliefs, and need to sustain their way of life. They lived with a consciousness of their *oneness*, as well as the oneness of all things around them.

They generally lived in harmony with each other, interacting mostly in a mutually beneficial fashion. The emphasis was on their own cultural values, beliefs, and customs, maintaining these, and passing them on to the next generation.

Their cultures were founded on the principle of unity in homogeneity, or unity in sameness. They were primarily concerned with unity on the level of their own community, because that is what was foremost in their realm of consciousness.

Indigenous people intrinsically know they are an integral part of the natural world around them, and intentionally live in union with this natural order. Their spiritual beliefs and practices are woven into the very fabric of life, making all of creation, and every moment of every day, sacred to them. Living life as practical mystics, the unitive elements of their spirituality have endured in spite of widespread devastation, forced migration, and centuries of cultural pressure to abandon their traditional ways.

Going back to ancient times, and bridging the consciousness divide for millennia (see the Epilogue), indigenous worldviews, beliefs, ceremonies, and all other actions are meant to bring the whole being, and the entire community, into accord with natural unity. In the traditional Lakota belief, all creatures are seen as relatives: "Whenever we pray we always pray "*mitakuye oyasin,*" for all our relations. We pray for all of the black people, all the yellow people, all the white people, and all the red people. We pray for all our relations." This is oneness in action, a natural extension of their mystic nature.

The qualities that often define indigenous and traditional cultures (harmony, balance, morality, mutuality, stability, complementarity, and cooperation) have contributed in an essential way to the pattern that has sustained them. Traditions (based upon a firm foundation of values and beliefs) led to bonding, which led to solidification and internal strength, which led to the growth of internal complexity.

Understanding indigenous cultures and the primal worldview is particularly important because it offers us a glimpse into a holistic way of experiencing existence. What we see as "religion" or "spirituality" (most often a separate part of our lives in which we strive to become united with a higher will or purpose), does not have a distinct name or domain of life; it permeates all aspects of life for indigenous people. Simply being alive is being spiritual.

With this deep understanding of reality comes a responsibility that is especially relevant to our time. Indigenous beliefs retain the ancient knowledge that the Creator entrusted humans to be "the keepers of the earth." The ancestors were given "the wisdom about Nature, about the interconnectedness of all things, about balance and about living in harmony," and they saw "the secrets of Nature." The keepers of this wisdom recognize that it's time to share these secrets with all people of the earth, as indigenous spirituality holds important keys to our collective evolution and survival.

The second phase in our cultural evolution began as societies became more complex, with different cultures interacting and experiencing conflict with each other. Humanity's original consciousness of oneness was severely tested and challenged, eventually transforming our thinking into a pervasive consciousness of *duality* to reflect the introduction of greater chaos and struggle in our lives.

This shift in consciousness led to a very long and painful process playing out over many centuries, even millennia, as communities expanded, splintered, and recreated themselves into new and more diverse communities. Differences and struggles not only continued but also escalated, and oppressive leaders and institutions, as well as wars and genocide on all levels, emerged.

Diversity became a fact of life that fostered separation and inequity. Duality became the lens through which we have viewed everything since mass migrations began. It was as if there was a forced replacement of unity within, and loyalty to, one's known group as people were expected to express the same attitude toward a new and larger group that carried different and often foreign views and values.

This is also explained as a natural evolutionary progression moving from simple levels of interaction to more complex levels. As the Baha'i writings say, "Unity of family, of tribe, of city-state, and nation have been successively attempted and fully established. World unity is the goal toward which a harassed humanity is striving."

But this is not a smooth process; it also includes an important time of transition, stress, and disorder, a period of limbo between the old and the new. Between tribe and city-state, and between city-state and nation, for example, have been transitional, temporary periods characterized by chaos and conflict.

This phase of duality, or unwanted nonreciprocal pluralism, where distinct cultures interact, find what they think are important differences, but are

> *In the beginning was only Being,*
> *One without a second.*
> *Out of himself he brought forth the cosmos*
> *And entered into everything in it.*
> *There is nothing that does not come from him.*
> ~Chandogya Upanishad

nevertheless expected to get along, is characterized by separateness and collective disagreements. This has brought about a long history of oppression, prejudice, racism, armed conflicts, and war between various cultural and ethnic groups.

The process is always characterized by the ongoing interaction and struggle between the forces of conservatism and dynamism. The intention of keeping things the way they are inevitably leads to change, which may mean increased conflict and struggle until the change is integrated into a new cultural system, whether or not mutually welcomed by all. As we've seen, this can be a very long process. Today, this is playing out on the grandest scale, illustrated vividly by the Black Lives Matter movement and the various opposing movements created in its wake.

The sequence of this unfoldment is unmistakable on the global level. While some factions within nations resist, the world moves onward toward its unification. This next step in humanity's evolution will bring us to our destined climax. As the Baha'i writings affirm, "A world, growing to maturity, must...recognize the oneness and wholeness of human relationships, and establish once and for all the machinery that can best incarnate this fundamental principle of its life."

Third, out of necessity for our collective survival, we are now in the midst of the slow but inevitable process of reclaiming our consciousness of *oneness*. The transformation humanity is currently undergoing is evident in notions such as global consciousness, global economy, and world citizenship. These are the natural outcomes of where our process of evolution has been leading us. Living with the realization of our interdependency as one human community with one common heritage and destiny is the only sustainable worldview left for us to embrace.

This would complete the basic pattern of the collective evolution of humanity over our long history, the return to where we began, to *oneness*, or unity, but on an inclusive level. The pattern as a whole can thus be described as: *oneness followed by duality followed by oneness*, or unity of the group followed by the plurality of many groups followed by the unity of humankind.

These three stages can be further defined as inherent unity, followed by a transitional period of disunity, followed by intended unity. The intended unity we are faced with at this time in our evolution is a deep understanding, acceptance, and putting into action of the concept of unity in diversity on its largest scale.

"Unity in Diversity" is not just a slogan or a buzz phrase. It's a way of explaining the principle of the oneness of humanity. It honors all the natural and unique forms of diversity that exist within the human family, from every ethnic group to each individual temperament. Diversity in the cultural and personal realms is just as vital and essential to the well-being of humanity as it is in the realm of the human gene pool. Putting the concept of unity in diversity into action would call for a wider loyalty, a broadening of affiliations without giving up any legitimate allegiances, and subordinating national interests for the greater good of a unified world.

This third stage, global unity in diversity, depends on the encouragement of the full participation of all groups and individuals in the life of the world community and the protection of the immense diversity of the human family. It would even become "a moral responsibility" to nurture and safeguard diversity.

To recap the pattern of our collective evolution, inherent unity is family and tribal unity, unity on the level of the most basic human unit. Intended unity is universal unity, on the largest possible scale. Yet only when we have achieved our intended unity on the universal level, will we recognize that that, too, is part of our inherent unity. Unity on this highest level is learned, and requires an acceptance of the concept of unity in diversity.

Evidence of this pattern in our evolution toward a global consciousness is also seen in a thread running throughout the field of psychology. Wilhelm Wundt, founder of experimental psychology and pioneer in social psychology, outlined in his 1912 book, *Elements of Folk Psychology*, the four stages of the cultural, social, religious, and psychological development of mankind from *Primitive Man*, the childhood of humanity's evolution, to *The Totemic Age*, the era of the symbolic world, to *The Heroic Age*, when community concerns give way to national concerns, to *The Development to Humanity*, when national affiliations give way to world-wide humanistic concerns.

For Wundt, "humanity" is a value-attribute referring to ethical characteristics that transcend "the limits of all more restricted associations, such as family, tribe, or State," and in which the individual's "appreciation of human worth shall have become a universal norm." This evolution does not "entail the disappearance of previous conditions," but "humanitarian culture takes...firmer root."

Wundt outlined four steps leading toward world consciousness. The first, the rise of *world empires*, "involves the conscious idea of a unity embracing the whole of mankind." The second step, *world culture*, results in an interest in humanity as a whole. In the third step, *world religion*, "we find religions that lay claim to being universal" in which national traits become secondary to universal characteristics. Finally, world culture and world religion form the basis for the fourth step leading to a global consciousness, or *world history*, in which there is "the historic consciousness of...the idea of mankind as a unity." These four steps represent humanity's conscious evolution toward the recognition of its own unity, or oneness.

It is quite remarkable how well Wundt's stages and steps fit our actual experience. While there are still strong inclinations in certain places to hold firmly to national concerns, we can also recognize very pronounced leanings toward seeing humanity as a whole. This became evident just a few years after Wundt wrote about his stages, with the inception of the League of Nations, and was undeniable by the end of the Second World War, when the United Nations came into being, though there remained pockets resisting this shift.

C.G. Jung, who could be seen as a spiritual or psychological descendent of Wilhelm Wundt, came soon after with his concept of the collective unconscious, which he said contains the whole spiritual heritage of humanity's evolution born anew in the mind of every individual. Thus, a pre-existent, inherited psychic system consisting of human universals move upward from an inner core of unconscious energy, through human ancestors to ethnic groups to national groups, and from tribe to family, and finally to the individual human psyche at the most conscious level.

Interestingly, both Wundt and Jung talk about the same goal, the psychic unity of mankind, yet have opposite ways of achieving it. Wundt sees it as an external, social process, Jung an internal, personal process. Merging what each is saying, they describe two different but essential parts to the same process. We are both *born with* the awareness of our oneness, *and* we gradually *move toward* a consciousness of this through the stages of our personal and collective evolution. Each type of awareness recognizes that inherent unity (collective unconscious) and intended unity (social consciousness) are both essential in achieving the goal of our collective evolution.

Following this thread in psychology through the 20th century, Erik Erikson's core concept of identity offers another perspective on the evolution of consciousness. Building his original theory of life cycle development around the task of identity formation in adolescence, he later moved from the personal sphere to the social sphere when he spoke about "man's wider, more inclusive identity." Erikson says mankind's task now is to move beyond an identity built upon exclusivity and superiority, representative of its collective adolescence, to one more fitting of its approaching maturity, by creating "a new and all-human identity."

The principle of conscious evolution affirms that there is a consciousness to evolution that is purposeful, directional, and progressive. Conscious evolution also widens the scope of justice to a unified and universal level of justice on a global scale.

Justice as the Cornerstone of an Ever-Advancing Civilization

A close look at the world's sacred traditions reveals a common thread of unity running throughout their core. This common thread is most evident in the Golden Rule, a universal expression at the heart of all spiritual truth, the most basic human value, and a basis for the principle of interconnectedness. It is known, understood, and accepted worldwide as an essential ethical and moral injunction.

But only as we look at the various expressions of the Golden Rule chronologically does it become evident that it is even about justice. Among the first expressions were, from the Hindu tradition, "This is the sum of duty: do naught unto others which would cause you pain if done to you;" and, from the Jewish faith, "What is hateful to you, do not do to your neighbor."

Later expressions were, from the Buddhist tradition: "Hurt not others in ways you yourself would find hurtful;" from the Christian faith: "In everything do to others as you would have them do to you;" and, from the faith of Islam: "Not one of you is a believer until he loves for his brother what he loves for himself."

These are all core spiritual, ethical, and moral injunctions, but not until the most recent Revelation, from the Baha'i Faith, is it clear what the real context of the Golden Rule is: "If thine eyes be turned towards *justice*, choose thou for thy neighbor that which thou choosest for thyself." The Golden Rule is justice in action.

The Golden Rule, a foundation *and* framework for a principle of justice that is universally shared, expresses the deepest aspirations of humanity: "the sum of all righteousness" in the Hindu tradition; "the whole of the Torah" in the Jewish faith; "the sum total of all righteousness" in the Buddhist tradition; "the one principle upon which one's whole life may proceed" in the Confucian tradition; "the law" in Christianity; and, "the noblest expression of religion" in the Muslim tradition.

But it is not specifically identified as the foundation for a principle of justice until Baha'u'llah's Revelation, in the mid-nineteenth century. Has justice evolved over the centuries, keeping up with changing times?

All indications are that our understanding of justice evolves as social interactions become more complex, *as well as* through the release of spiritual energies in each age. The Golden Rule is now the basis for a system of global justice.

Justice, the sign of compassion in action in the world, finds its fulfillment in a standard of unconditional love. This is the one means capable of creating global harmony. A universal system of global justice—a standard of equity and fairness implying no preferential treatment *and* ultimate regard for the welfare of humanity as a single community—is a prerequisite for the realization of the promise of world peace.

Justice, too, has its own evolutionary path, or developmental stages. A few millennia of societies characterized by limited, inequitable, and incomplete justice systems have given way to an age of social justice on the largest scale possible. Following universal human rights, it is no longer acceptable not to have an inclusive, equitable global system of justice.

What was seen as justice, or even a "right," in 1790 may not be appropriate today. We have made great strides toward cultural and social equity; yet we still have quite a ways to go in achieving universal human rights in all aspects of life.

With each domain of human rights achieving an equitable stature in society, another domain rises to the surface. Economic justice, in the form of the Occupy Movement, has become the much-needed social rallying cry of the 2nd decade of the 21st century, thrusting the spiritual principle of the elimination of extremes of poverty and wealth to the forefront of all injustices facing humanity.

Poverty is now understood as but one symptom of an out-of-balance, unjust system of social and economic relationships that promote the interests of a few over the many. Remedies to this social ill must address the harmful "values" at the center of those attitudes, behaviors, and decisions that contribute to economic injustices.

Global poverty, and its related problems, like AIDS, have become recognized for what they are: everyone's concern everywhere in the world, as musician and social activist Bono emphasized in his 2005 TED talk: "This is about justice... The fact that ours is the first generation that can look disease and extreme poverty in the eye, look across the ocean to Africa, and say this, and mean it, 'We do not have to stand for this. A whole continent written off—We don't have to stand for this.'"

One approach that is playing an effective role in establishing justice as the framework for human relationships is a human rights approach, one that establishes and maintains "rights" for all human beings while guaranteeing a moral foundation of mutual and equitable trusteeship between all individuals and disallowing both a rampant individualism and the elevation of the state or any group above others.

Another central guiding principle of the human rights approach would be the equality of women and men. The dire condition of women—including girls and elder women—in all aspects of human life needs to be attended to, in order to ensure justice for women economically, socially, and at all levels of governance. Equal rights and participation of women in legal, political, economic, academic, social and artistic endeavors is a prerequisite for a just and more peaceful society.

If the world's leaders grasped the principle of the oneness of humanity as the operational principle on all levels of society, and reshaped the structures of governance to reflect it, the world's major injustices—like genocide and terrorism—could be eliminated. Living according to the principle of oneness is a prerequisite to justice in its fullest expression, which is a prerequisite to peace.

The full benefits of social justice will not be realized until justice is seen as a human capacity housed within the human soul, a gift meant to be shared.

Justice and equity are twin pillars protecting the wellbeing of the peoples of the world. Social justice, fair-mindedness, compassion, generosity, consideration for others, and loving-kindness are divine attributes and qualities, part of our common spiritual heritage.

Acting toward all beings with a sense of equity, we come to understand justice not through the eyes of someone else, but through our own independent investigation; and, we discover that the essence of divine wisdom and grace is justice itself. It is through this discerning eye that we ultimately see with the eye of oneness.

Today, more than ever, we need champions of justice, equity, kindness, and unconditional love, who see first see the same virtues of nobility in every human being. As understood by the world's sacred traditions, justice is the embodiment of divine order on earth. Justice opens hearts, reveals secrets of the soul, prepares the way for unity, and leads to the wellbeing of humanity. No power can stand up to the force of justice. It is the true transformer of society, what will lead to lasting peace.

Justice is the equalizer in human affairs; it can moderate the extremes of wealth and poverty, create equality between women and men, and remove the hurdles of national rivalries, prejudice, religious strife, economic barriers, and class distinctions. This transformation of society is the most-needed community building of our time.

Required for this fundamental change of consciousness is a wholehearted embrace of the primary principle of our time, the oneness of humanity, which further requires laying aside self-interests, serving the common good, and contributing to the advancement of oppressed peoples. Yet, this is the only thing that will awaken latent spiritual capacities within us and change this world into a new world.

Justice is the unifying force expressed in every dimension of reality. The Baha'i writings affirm, "The light of men is justice, quench it not with the contrary winds of oppression and tyranny. Justice is a powerful force. It is the…standard-bearer of love and bounty…The purpose of justice is the appearance of unity among men…No radiance can compare with that of justice." This is the promise of justice.

Justice has been long evolving toward wholeness and unity. Actually, our understanding of justice, and our capacity to carry it out, has evolved and expanded with each and every social advance we take toward oneness. As our circles of unity become wider and wider, the effects of justice carried out become deeper and deeper.

However, with the punitive system of justice we have lived by for many centuries now, we have not been able to experience the fullest effects of our growing circles of unity. The "eye for an eye" and a "life for a life" system, along with the extremes of unbridled genocide and war, have created the need for restorative justice, which adds generations on to the process of achieving true justice.

Again, indigenous cultures, by experiencing a living web of interconnections within their communities for a long time, have had a built-in system of restorative justice simultaneously offering meaningful support to victims *and* helping perpetrators restore harmony in the community. This is a model that can be writ large.

Because our consciousness has evolved to a level of maturity, the world community desperately needs a unitive system of justice, designed explicitly to maintain unity on all levels, built upon the standard of compassion, respect, and equity for all human beings, and with the ability to restore harmony built right in to the system. This, too, requires seeing through the eye of oneness, shifting our consciousness to see the whole first, rather than to give preference to any of its parts.

Love *and* justice combined results in unity right away, rather than needing more energy later on to restore another injustice. Justice is the greatest need of our time because world unity is necessary for our very survival. The fate of humanity in the 21st century depends upon the twin forces of love and justice bringing about equitable relationships on all levels.

There is a hidden wholeness to all of existence that a system of global justice has to take into account. As the declaration of the 1993 Parliament of the World's Religions made clear, "We are interdependent...We must sink our narrow differences for the cause of world community...We commit ourselves to a culture of non-violence, respect, justice, and peace... We must strive for a just social and economic order, in which everyone has an equal chance to reach full potential as a human being...Let no one be deceived, there is no global justice without truthfulness and humanness."

To this, the following needs to be added: there can be no global justice without the recognition of the oneness of humanity. Carrying out global justice today based on oneness and interdependence is the only thing that will ensure the achievement of the purpose of justice: establishing unity in diversity, the most practical need of our time.

The collective transformation of the world depends ultimately and primarily upon this balanced and inclusive formulation of justice in the world. Through the power of faith in action, communities with the power to reshape the world can be built. In our time, world unity is the goal *and* the greatest need. A fully functioning and operating system of global justice is what will best get us there.

Part Two

The Nature of Transformation

All things are subject to transformation and change...
Creation is the expression of motion, and motion is life...
Nothing is stationary in the material world of outer phenomena
or in the inner world of intellect and consciousness.

-Abdu'l-Baha

To cease moving
and no longer be torn by the tensions between opposites
is equivalent to no longer existing in the Cosmos.

-Mircea Eliade

The upheaval of our world
and the upheaval in consciousness is one and the same...
We are only at the threshold
of a new spiritual epoch.

-C.G. Jung

Principle 4

Unity is the result of the conscious confrontation of opposing forces

Human beings possess a consciousness designed to confront and overcome difficulties and challenges. Even when tested to our limits, we are built to push beyond those apparent limits and enter unknown realms. Trials and tribulations are therefore purposive; they are a bounty of divine bestowal meant to help facilitate the process of transformation. They become the cause of great advancement.

Opposition creates opportunity, is essential in maintaining the law of balance in the universe, and is necessary for ensuring cyclical progress within a linear process. Opposing forces in our lives exist to take us beyond their duality (which represents separation and temporality) to experience a deeper unity. Our unique capacity of consciousness allows us to merge opposites into a hidden whole (which represents a timeless reality).

When we restore the dualities to their whole, when we consciously merge opposing forces, when we shift our beliefs or views to the oneness that exists beyond separation, when the eternal is seen in the temporary, when the division between body, mind, and spirit is united, transformation occurs. Transformation is a necessary requisite for growth and evolution. All of this is as true on the collective level, for humanity as a whole, as it is on the personal, for the individual.

4

Opposition as the Catalyst for Transformation

Before the beginning of years
There came to the making of man
Time, with a gift of tears;
Grief, with a glass that ran;
Pleasure, with pain for leaven;
Summer, with flowers that fell;
Remembrance, fallen from heaven,
And madness risen from hell;
Strength without hands to smite;
Love that endures for a breath;
Night, the shadow of light,
And life, the shadow of death.

-A.C. Swinburne

We live in a time when change is happening at a perilous pace. What we think we know of the past is being replaced or challenged by an endless flow of new information. Dramatic discoveries revealing hidden mysteries and technological advances enabling instantaneous global communication are increasing every day, forever altering the way we live and carry out our lives. The world is being reformed and transformed before our very eyes.

With this rapid increase of inventions and other advancements of all kinds, it feels like change itself is changing. Each step up the ladder of evolution has quickened the pace of the ascent, making the entire progression seem more and more at risk, and the need for a deep level transformation on both the personal and collective more imminent.

In the words of one current observer, "A relentless and accelerating tide of change has swept across the globe, transforming daily life, throwing together populations who previously cared little about or for each other, altering human and political relationships, and greatly improving material well-being, but at the same time threatening us with the disruption of established social orders and the possibility of cataclysm and extinction."

We seem to be in the adolescent phase of our collective development, moving toward a more mature outlook when we will consciously act as one human family sharing one planet. Even as we struggle to overcome our child-like tendencies as a species, we know we are headed in that direction.

As the Baha'i writings emphasize, "Far from signalizing the end of civilization, the convulsive changes towards which humanity is being ever more rapidly impelled will serve to release the 'potentialities inherent in the station of man' and reveal 'the full measure of his destiny on earth, the innate excellence of his reality.'" This level of confidence is warranted today because "All the signs indicate that a sea change in human consciousness is under way." We are clearly in transformational times.

The Polarity Principle

Helping to guide this process are essential opposing forces in life, a dialectic involving a give and take that is at one moment simple and straightforward and at another moment a core mystery of existence. Each day ends with darkness and begins with light. Fall follows summer. This ubiquitous dialectic creates a dynamic of opposition that is with us every day of our lives.

This dynamic shapes the most fundamental processes of human and social development, balancing stability and change, and guiding us to our fullest potential. There is a basic struggle within each stage of personal and collective development that creates an essential opposition designed to generate and facilitate growth.

Life is made up of an ongoing series of contradictory struggles meant to move us along the developmental path we were designed to move along. Development could not happen without the tension that forms the core of the pattern of transformation. This pattern (*birth/death/rebirth* or *separation/initiation/return*) is built into traditional rites of passage, and is found in the sacred stories of the world's myths and religions.

Transformation is the nature of life. The nature of transformation is destruction (breaking down) followed by construction (building up), or disintegration followed by integration.

> *Perhaps there is a pattern set up in the heavens for one who desires to see it,*
> *and having seen it, to find one in himself.*
> ~Plato

Change and transformation on the physical plane is ongoing, built in to our make-up, and inherent to life on both the personal and collective levels.

Transformation is how we access the higher levels of human consciousness, and the hidden mysteries of life. It is the way we satisfy the insatiable hunger in our souls that draws us ever closer to an eternal realm. Change is usually slow and gradual. The key to true transformation is a quantum-leap shift in consciousness where things aren't simply recombined but something new appears for the first time.

Swinburne's verse at the beginning of the chapter illustrates perfectly a principle that seems to be a fundamental law of nature. Endless pairs of opposites create contradictions and conflicts between each part, yet they are at the same time complementary. Opposites are both contradictory and complementary.

This understanding goes way back. From the 15th century B.C., the Bhagavad-Gita says, "In this world, Being is twofold: the Divided, the Undivided. All things that live are "the Divided." That which sits apart, "the Undivided." And, from the 5th century B.C., Heraclitus, said, "The way up and the way down are one and the same."

From a holistic perspective, the opposites are not divided at all. Heraclitus said, "It is sickness that makes health pleasant...weariness precedes rest, hunger brings on plenty and evil leads to good." He is noting, as did Swinburne, the contradictions that are at the same time complementary. Recognizing the pattern here, and that there must be a principle to account for the paradoxes in life, is partly a matter of vantage point but more so a matter of consciousness.

The Yin-Yang symbol is a good example of how the meaning is in the whole and not its parts. Each part is has its existence only in relationship to the other. To see the meaning and purpose in oppositions, we have to be able to think more holistically, which is all the while possible with a consciousness of the whole.

The principle of polarity is also bound up in the concept of relativity. Would there be light without dark, up without down, good without evil? One is what it is only because of its relationship to the other. We can see both as opposites and contradictory, *and* we can see them as different aspects of a whole that are therefore ultimately complementary.

It helps, too, to see transformation, the process of the merging of polarities, as an archetype, or a universal and oft repeated process whose timeless elements are shared by myth, ritual, and religion, and found in our own lives, as well. An archetype is a pattern repeated because it is an essential aspect of human life that may need to be experienced many times to show us life's deepest meanings.

Archetypes are latent potentialities, or pattern-forming elements, residing in the human psyche, the meaning-making part of our vast store of ancestral knowledge about the profound relations between the Creator, man, and the cosmos. They remain unconscious until our own real life experiences bring them forth into consciousness, making our individual experience part of the universal human experience.

When a latent archetype passes into consciousness it is felt as an illumination, or a revelation. An archetype is the original form of a *type* of experience from which all other forms of that experience follow and are copied, a recurring 'mythological component,' a *type* of a common situation, or a *type* of universal figure, what we would think of as a literary motif that is part of our inherited humanity.

Examples of such potentially transformational archetypal situations would be "the hero's quest," "the battle for deliverance from the mother," or "the night sea journey." Archetypal figures include the divine child, the trickster, or the wise old man. They all carry the power to influence, awaken, and therefore transform us.

Archetypes keep us in the nourishing riverbed through which the water of life has flowed for centuries by connecting us to the timelessness of human experience and digging a deep channel into the soul of our existence. The interplay of their inherent oppositions creates a moment of the merging of opposites, which is the act of transformation. The archetype thus carries a "healing" function and is felt as "numinous," or as having a profound spiritual significance.

The Necessity of Adversity

In this physical, temporal plane, change is inevitable, but transformation is conditional upon our conscious understanding of the intended meaning and purpose the transition has for us. Transformation depends upon and incorporates adversity (a central component of socially prescribed transitions like traditional rites of passage) because this creates and amplifies the necessary polarity, or opposition.

The goal of the transformation process is not the uncertainty or chaos that initially arises from the adversity, but the synthesis and union of seemingly separate parts when they are recognized as a whole. Being able to see the whole in the midst of apparent opposition is a great help in enabling the transformation to occur.

This essential oppositional process makes up a divine pattern that we can depend upon. Sacred scriptures worldwide indicate how transformation is designed to re-make the character of human beings from physical to spiritual beings. In Christianity, we find "And we all, with unveiled face, beholding the glory of the Lord, are changed into his likeness" (2 Corinthians 3:18).

In the Baha'i Faith, transformations are linked directly to an experience of opposing forces: "Know ye that trials and tribulations have, from time immemorial, been the lot of the chosen Ones of God and His beloved... Such is God's method carried into effect of old, and such will it remain in the future. Blessed are the steadfastly enduring, they that are patient under ills and hardships, who lament not over anything that befall them." No one escapes the hardships brought on by the clash of opposites; they define the process of transformation.

Transformation is not an accident; it is essential to ongoing progress in the physical world. Abdu'l-Baha makes this clear, "Change and transformation are necessities of the contingent world" but "not of the Essence of Divinity." Only in this temporal realm of the ever-changing physical world, and in the inner world of consciousness, is transformation necessary and repeated many times over; in the eternal realm of the spirit it is not, due to its "indivisible oneness."

Thus, it is within our human capabilities to merge such opposites, and restore them to the hidden whole they already are. Recognizing that wholeness is the nature of Reality, we move along a continuum of awareness in steps and stages.

The essential oppositions, and the nature of transformation itself, can best be narrowed down to the core opposition of *light* and *shadow*. Light, an ancient symbol representing the qualities of radiance, sanctity, love, justice, and every spiritual attribute that emanates from divinity, is central to the world's sacred traditions.

As it is said in the Bhagavad-Gita, "The Light of Lights He is, in the heart of the Dark shining eternally;" in Genesis (1:3-4), "And God said, Let there be light and there was light. And God divided the light from the darkness;" and, in the Qur'an (24:35), "God is the light of the heavens and of the earth." We are most in need of acquiring the attributes of light.

Though we have light all around us, *and* within us, we live in the shadow world, and the shadow world lives within us, too. Shadow, in the psychology of C. G. Jung, represents an archetypal image of the hidden, repressed, or unknown, which heightens even more the level of adversity we face in this world of illusion. Universal shadow tendencies (violence, crime, cruelty) exist in everyone. But only when "the creative interrelationship of light and shadow is accepted and lived as the foundation of this world is life in this world truly possible for man." The shadow is "the paradoxical secret of transformation itself."

Both parts of the whole—light *and* shadow (or grace *and* adversity)—are necessary for transformation. Things are most sharply measured or defined by their opposites. Would we recognize what it means to be healthy if we knew nothing of sickness? Would the Easter story be complete without Jesus's betrayal at the hand of Judas? Would poverty be an injustice without the existence of wealth? A conscious life finds meaning in these contrasts that impact and even transforms us.

This law of opposition is key to understanding the process of transformation. As Jung says, "There is no balance, no system of self-regulation, without opposition...Nothing so promotes the growth of consciousness as this inner confrontation of opposites...Only here, in life on earth, where opposites clash together, can the general level of consciousness be raised... That is probably why earthly life is of such great significance, and why it is that what a human being "brings over" at the time of death is so important." The "tension of opposites which seek compensation in unity" brings about the all-important expansion of consciousness.

Within this context of necessary opposition, nothing is extra or superfluous. Everything on the path is seen as sacred. Everything has a lesson to teach us, even "mistakes." As it is said in the Native American tradition, "Whenever the Creator gives you something, don't hesitate. Grab it."

We therefore need to be conscious to be able to move out of the shadow, resolve any tension that comes our way, or to recognize grace when it arrives, as it often shows up when we need it most, but least expect it.

Grace can be essential in resolving the conflict of opposites. A parallel to the mythological motif of "supernatural aid" which comes at crucial points in the hero's journey to assist the transformation process when it appears at a dead-end, grace is an assurance of protection and guidance, that we are never alone, and that we are in harmony with the forces of the universe. But everything can be seen as grace, too.

As catalysts for our continued growth and transformation, opposition and adversity can be tests coming from the material world to teach us precisely what we need to release in order to become more attached to the spiritual realm.

Abdu'l-Baha clarifies this concept. "Grief and sorrow do not come to us by chance, they are sent to us by the Divine Mercy for our own perfecting."

Grasping the spiritual meaning of adversity helps us recognize that there is a resolution to the seeming paradox of suffering in the world. It is suffering only if that is all we see it as.

Knowing the purpose of adversity helps us recognize it as a great tool of personal and collective transformation. This physical world is designed to promote both our physical and spiritual growth. It is an illusion that this physical world is all there is. By it we gradually become aware that we are essentially spiritual beings. Our deepest, longest-lasting happiness lies in this expanded consciousness.

We have an innate need and capacity to overcome and resolve the difficulties and adversities we encounter. The pattern of transformation exists to maintain a balance between opposites and to show that there is an underlying order to such disorder. On the collective level, these natural, normal, and necessary contrasts are becoming more and more pronounced.

The Dark Night of the Collective Soul

It is well known from the world's spiritual, mystical, and religious literature that we experience periods of doubt, confusion, and conflict many times over in our lives, all of which can fuel a dark night that eventually turns into a process of transformation.

The dark night is a fitting metaphor of life's crises and the *muddle* or initiation phase of the universal pattern designed to bring about transformation in our lives. The journey into a dark night where all is new, unknown, and at risk, is a journey toward reshaping our lives, and redefining who we are.

Introduced by 16th-century mystic St. John of the Cross, the phrase "dark night of the soul" identifies a time of challenge, despair, and spiritual crisis in a person's life that sometimes becomes a portal leading to a transformation that involves a symbolic death and rebirth experience resulting in a deeper spiritual life. This motif fills classic literature; countless heroes and heroines have made it through a dark tunnel and come out the other side experiencing their own transformation.

Relatively easy to understand on the individual level, what about the dark night of the *collective* soul? Is there a similar process leading to the death and rebirth of the community, the nation, or the entire human society as a whole?

Is humanity currently experiencing a loss of soul, a spiritual crisis? Civilizations and empires have long followed a pattern of rise and fall, bringing to mind the Egyptian, Aztec, Incan, Mayan, Greek, Roman, Persian, and Ottoman empires, and in more recent centuries even Spain, Portugal, France, Holland, and Great Britain. All these powers have risen and fallen, yet continued to exist in a different form after their dark night of the collective soul. The pattern they all followed is one of birth-death-rebirth.

Many feel we, humanity as a whole, are currently in that dark night of the collective soul. In our time, the transformation of one leads inevitably to the transformation of all. What affects the part, impacts the whole.

However, even though we are becoming a global community, a "dark night" in one region of the world does not mean ultimately that transformation will occur in all regions of the globe at the same time. Global transformation would be a gradual, part-by-part process, in the long run resulting in the advancement of civilization as a whole.

All of creation is part of this divine pattern of opposition followed by progress. Nothing escapes the cycle of opposites that defines the nature and process of change and growth. It is a process of deep organic change in the structure of society that most characterizes the dark night of the collective soul.

A "two-fold process" of "universal fermentation" in every continent and every sphere of life (religious, social, economic or political) is, according to Shoghi Effendi, "purging and reshaping humanity in anticipation of the Day when the wholeness of the human race will have been recognized and its unity established."

This dual process is part of a collective pattern of growth characterized by "a series of pulsations, of alternating crises and triumphs," forming "a dialectic of victory and crisis." One aspect of the process is essentially integrative, striving to unify world systems, while the other is fundamentally disruptive, tending to oftentimes violently maintain the barriers that separate humanity, keeping it from its destined goal.

Ours is a time of one of humanity's greatest transformations. We live in a world defined by the dramatic collapse of the old forms of society. This disintegrating force has made chaos the norm for the generations of the 20th and 21st centuries. Though this societal fermentation is a painful process, all of the elements that have been broken apart will gradually be reorganized and reformed into something entirely new.

Humanity's story has taken this turn toward chaos and disintegration because it refuses to acknowledge and embrace the spiritually-based principles meant to guide its own evolution into a new global era that demands cooperation and integration. This shortsighted and limited vision is holding humanity hostage.

At the same time, a vast process of renewal is underway throughout the world. Our suffering is serving to purify and bring together the entire human race. Our dark night is changing us from one state of being to another. This is an inescapable part of our healing and rebirth.

The way forward may be through further pain and destruction. Yet this is what will finally bring the differences into sharper focus and help us learn to distinguish more clearly between poison and honey, dark and light, and illusion and reality.

In fact, as the recurring crises increase and intensify all around us, it is most important to maintain a focus on the whole overarching process that is indeed unfolding. The Baha'i writings provide this big picture, long-term perspective:

"The winds of despair are, alas, blowing from every direction, and the strife that divides and afflicts the human race is daily increasing… adversities unimaginably appalling, undreamed of crises and upheavals… might well combine to engrave in the soul of an unheeding generation those truths and principles which it has disdained to recognize and follow… Whether peace is to be reached only after unimaginable horrors precipitated by humanity's stubborn clinging to old patterns of behavior, or is to be embraced now by an act of consultative will, is the choice before all who inhabit the earth… The current world confusion and calamitous condition in human affairs [is a] natural phase in an organic process leading ultimately and irresistibly to the unification of the human race in a single social order whose boundaries are those of the planet."

The promise of world peace has been out there for millennia; it is up to us – now – to bring it into reality. As a glimmer of the light at the end of the dark night begins to rise above the horizon, we can keep our eyes much more on this coming dawn, and on the signs of hope and progress we are witnessing.

A World Giving Birth

We are at the end of one cycle and the beginning of another, witnessing the death of the old and the birth of the new. As Jung noted some eighty years ago, "It seems to me that we are only at the threshold of a new spiritual epoch." We are the midwives not of a physical birth, but a profound spiritual birth, as Teilhard de Chardin makes clear, "We are watching the birth, more than the death, of a World."

We are at what Ervin Laszlo calls the "tipping point," where we head toward mass extinction or a sustainable future. Can we head any further down the "path to breakdown" without it being too late, or will we wake up and head down the "path to breakthrough"? It may just be that we are already far enough into the birth process that there is no turning back.

How can we not move toward "breakthrough" when we are more conscious every day that we are deeply connected to each other? Conscious activism in every realm is evident. The desire for a peaceful and sustainable world is influencing the way we think, act, *and* the way we are growing.

The eventual result of this imminent birth process, as Laszlo describes it, will be "a consciousness that recognizes our connections to each other and to the cosmos...a consciousness of connectedness and memory... [that] conveys a sense of belonging, ultimately, of oneness... a wellspring of empathy with nature and solidarity among people."

People around the world are embracing world-shaping trends that are leading the way in this birthing process. Laszlo says, "An individual endowed with planetary consciousness recognizes his or her role in the evolutionary process and acts responsibly in light of this perception." He defines planetary consciousness as "the knowing as well as the feeling of the vital interdependence of and essential oneness of humankind, and the conscious adoption of the ethics and the ethos that this entails."

Futurist Barbara Marx Hubbard also uses the birthing metaphor to describe this moment in our conscious evolution. We are in the midst of a great shift in bringing about the planetary birth. The crises we are facing are essential to the process, just as birth pangs are to being born. Crises are evolutionary drivers of the rebirth process, accelerating the spiritual development of humanity.

Archbishop Desmond Tutu says, "The atomized homogeneous groups that existed in the past are no longer the truth of our world. We must recognize that we are part of one group, one family – the human family. Our survival as a planet depends on it. We are part of one family, and we are fundamentally good."

The transformation process described here, essentially a symbolic death of the old way of seeing the world followed by the birth of a new worldview, has long been underway. James Redfield and Michael Murphy have outlined the continuity in the great turning-points of the evolution of consciousness, beginning with our ancestors who awoke to the Transcendent through shamanism and the ancient mystery schools, to the founding and flourishing of each of the world's great religious traditions (East and West from Hinduism to Islam), followed by the Renaissance and finally the Enlightenment and the Scientific Revolution taking us into the 18th century.

Another "turning point" soon after this that is either overlooked or as yet unknown in this process of collective transformation, but is considered by many as when the rebirth process itself began, is the Revelation of Baha'u'llah in the mid-19th century. Could this have been the spark that ignited the "clarifying and unifying vision capable of transcending irresolvable religious conflicts"? Could the recent scientific and spiritual advances, and other far reaching changes the world has witnessed since then, be part of this release of creative energies?

Though smaller in numbers than other world religions, with 7.5 million followers, the Baha'i Faith has expanded worldwide more rapidly than any other tradition, and is now the second most widespread religion in the world. Its teachings and universal spiritual principles have appealed to people of all backgrounds. People who follow the mystical traditions within the world's religions (such as Kabbalah, Sufism, and Contemplative Christianity) as well as Indigenous peoples around the world resonate deeply with its primary emphasis on unity and oneness.

Profound changes certainly have taken place throughout the world since the beginning of this rebirth process that has borne much pain in all realms of civil life. Convulsions in society, fierce antagonisms among the entire range of identity groups representing the peoples of the world, the downfall of kings, the collapse of nations, the extinction of dynasties, the deterioration of time-honored institutions, world wars, and the rise of fanatical terrorism are all evidences of the travail that has characterized the slow but inevitable symbolic death of an aging civilization.

At the same time, a new consciousness of oneness is laboring to be born. Bearing the seed of a new world civilization, the Revelation of Baha'u'llah has as its foundation what have since become the core principles of our time: that one single Divine Being, known by hundreds of names, such as Brahman, Yahweh, God, and Allah, whose ultimate nature is unknowable, created the universe and all creatures and forces within it; that from this Supreme Being have flowed a continuous succession of Prophets to guide humanity toward understanding reality, around whom have formed the world's religions and spiritual traditions; that all humanity is part of one human family; that, with only one reality, the discoveries and findings of science must be in harmony with the principles and beliefs of revealed religion, and vice versa; that the full equality and partnership of women and men is essential to human progress; that prejudice – whether racial, ethnic, national, religious, or economic – must be overcome if humanity is to establish a just global society; that there is an essential connection between equitable economic prosperity and the spiritual principles governing life; that without preconceptions we must acquire knowledge through our own efforts by independently investigating truth; and, that the longed-for goal of world peace, now the greatest need of our time, is within our reach.

Though it has taken us nearly a century and three quarters to get to this point of near-universal awareness of these principles, and though we are still awaiting the final shift in consciousness to bring this understanding into full acceptance and practice, we can find motivation and renewed energy in witnessing the widespread change that has and is continuously occurring in these directions in the world.

If we could see with the eye of the Creator, we would see the present politically disrupted, economically paralyzed, and socially writhing world slowly but ultimately breaking up, preparing the way for the birth of the new world.

The evolutionary shift rate is speeding up, yet we cannot say when the birth process will finally be completed. Nor do we know for sure whether the just and equitable global society sought for by so many for so long will be achieved only after further unimaginable horrors resulting from blindly clinging to old patterns, or more quickly and smoothly by consciously embracing and acting upon the newly revealed spiritual principles of our time.

What we do know is that the choice is fully ours. It is a gradual and unfolding process of evolution that guides our collective progress in assuming responsibility and actively carrying forward an ever-advancing civilization.

The world is birthing a whole new way of seeing the world. We are in the midst of a transformation of consciousness never before witnessed. Spiritual energies that have already been released will ensure the renewal of individuals and institutions, opening the way for a higher order of organization and well-being on earth. As Baha'u'llah said, "The object of every Revelation" is to "effect a transformation in the whole character of mankind, a transformation that shall manifest itself outwardly and inwardly, that shall affect both its inner life and external conditions."

Part Three

The Nature of Reality

Reality is one; and when found, it will unify all mankind.
Reality is the knowledge of God... reality underlies all the great religious
systems of the world.

-Abdu'l-Baha

All will be well,
and you yourself shall see
that every manner of thing will be well.

-Julian of Norwich

One cannot help but be in awe when he contemplates the mysteries of eternity,
of life, of the marvelous structure of reality.

-Albert Einstein

Principle 5

Reality is one, and global harmony is inevitable

Reality is a changeless, grand organic whole; every thing in it is connected to – and part of – every other thing. Our conscious evolution is purposeful, and has been leading us closer and closer to this understanding of the oneness that is indivisible. It has taken us through stages, from family to tribe to city-state to national unity; now we are on the verge of realizing world unity, as one human family.

The promised day is upon us. This is the day processes set in motion millennia ago guided us to. Not only do all the world's spiritual and religious traditions look forward to some form of "a new heaven and earth," there has always been the hope and desire for "peace on earth."

The most recent of these sacred traditions, the Baha'i Faith, boldly asserts that world peace is not only a promise waiting to be fulfilled, but is also inevitable. This does not mean we sit back and watch. Rather, this view renews hope, affirms the eventual outcome, acknowledges a purpose to these turbulent and chaotic times, and raises a call to action – because the way we get to this desired outcome is dependent upon us. With this vision of the future, and knowing that the human race will not be obliterated, we must take on our responsibility as proactive midwives to shorten this painful transition period and bring about a gentle as possible rebirth of the planet. Most vital is assisting this process with our own sacred activism every day of our lives, applying the wisdom, practices, and tools already available to us.

5

Spiritual Forces Guiding Us Toward Unity

As all things originate from one Essence,
so they are developing according to one law, and they are destined to one aim.
-The Gospel of Buddha

Whatever is isolated is confusing.
Wholeness alone is reliable and leads man to salvation.
-Martin Buber

Deep down the consciousness of mankind is one.
-David Bohm

The mystery of oneness is at the heart of creation. Material and spiritual reality, counter-balancing parts of the same unified reality, are energized and held together by the same force that has the same influence upon the entire universe. This connective, creative energy, known as Love, the divine spirit, or Grace, is the unifying force expressed in every dimension of reality.

By its very nature, Reality cannot be more than one; it is the absolute unity of all existence, the whole within which the great diversity of all its parts find their place. The existence of one reality has forever directed our collective evolution toward the realization of this oneness. Unity is the underlying principle defining reality.

Quantum theorists and the prophets of the world's religions alike support this truth. Spiritual truths, found everywhere in creation, are consistent across all levels. A relationship or pattern that exists in physical reality has a counterpart in the spiritual realm. The physical world is an expression of spirit, a reflection of the one reality.

As the Buddha indicates, all things originate from one Essence, develop according to one law, and are destined to one aim. We are being guided back toward our primordial consciousness of oneness.

Johanna Macy captures well this spirit of our age: "We are living cells in the living body of Earth." While our "collective body" is experiencing severe trauma on the outside, on the inner level our consciousness is "listening to a message from the universe." This is the same message that has been coming through to the mystics and prophets for centuries, now renewed and accessible to all.

Reality as a Continuum

For everything there is a continuum. The way we understand reality is no different. Reality is the mother of all other continuums. How we perceive reality is dependent upon where we are on our own consciousness continuum. Reality does not change, we do. As we change, we see the same reality differently.

Reality is the whole unified field comprising the entirety of creation; all of its parts fit together in a mysterious harmony, a hidden wholeness. But we discover the *reality* of reality gradually. Even though we originate from oneness, are born into a realm of dualities, and move back to a consciousness of oneness, "awareness is all that changes in the journey from separation to the one reality," as Deepak Chopra says.

Some understandings may only be possible from different vantage points further along the consciousness continuum, like seeing the sun rising in the east and setting in the west, or knowing that the sun does not rise but rather the earth turns. An evolving consciousness may be the most fulfilling potential we are born with.

Moving across the consciousness continuum from separation to unity allows us to see wholeness, to get the true picture of reality as it is. This shift can come as a sudden new awareness, but its total impact may not be fully experienced until we eventually let go of our attachment to duality.

Usually a gradual process, most children start out with limited access to reality. As our sensing, feeling, and mental capacities develop and mature, we grasp greater levels of complexity, think symbolically, understand other points of view, apply logic, weigh dichotomies, make difficult decisions, think abstractly and hypothetically, and eventually become theoretical about life and our experience of it. As our thinking matures, our consciousness expands, and we see what was once hidden.

One of the insights gained as we progress along this continuum is that Divine truth, along with scientific truth, is seen as relative, progressive, and unfolding gradually but continuously across time, just as consciousness unfolds and expands. Truth is not at once known and fixed for all time, but is rather revealed little by little, and when another piece of truth becomes apparent, yet another will follow, when the time or perspective to view it becomes available.

We can visualize the consciousness continuum by starting at a midpoint and moving in opposite directions, which in turn gives us opposing views of reality. In one direction, our view would be based on dualities and in the other direction on oneness. On the duality side of the continuum, reality is built upon the illusion of duality, dogmatic and exclusive principles, and engenders confusion, incomplete knowledge, irreverence, violence, fear, and attachment. It is ego-based and leads from stereotypes to bias to prejudice to oppression and racism, and ultimately to war. (See chart)

Moving in the other direction from the midpoint, toward oneness, a holistic view of reality is built upon wholeness and spiritual principles, engendering clarity, truth, knowledge, reverence for life, nonviolence, fearlessness, and nonattachment. It is spirit-based and leads from respect to appreciation to compassion to equality to cooperation and ultimately to unity and peace.

How The Consciousness Continuum Can Lead to Opposite Outcomes

The Attitudes, Values, and Principles We Live By
Determine Whether We End Up With Either War or Peace

Start With: **End With:**

A Pragmatic-Centered (leads to) >> Generalizations >> Stereotypes >> Bias >> Prejudice >> Oppression >> Racism >> <u>War</u>
Perspective

(An attitude or approach based on
practical or dogmatic needs or results.)

	oversimplification	segregation	discrimination	exploitation	violence
	bigotry	antipathy	conflict	marginalization	
categorization	discord	disputes	cruelty	powerlessness	destruction
DUALITY separation	gender inequality	hatred	cultural imperialism	terrorism	
difference	ethnocentrism	hierarchical statuses	fundamentalist movements	"religious" violence	
	in-groups/out-groups	economic extremes	territorial conquest	genocide	
	superior/inferior groups	secular nationalism	unbridled nationalism		
	dominant/subordinate groups			... *non-existence*	

Start With: **End With:**

A Principle-Centered (leads to) >> Respect >> Appreciation >> Equality >> Cooperation >> Unity >> <u>Peace</u>
Perspective

(An inner state supported by
a spiritual or moral attitude.)

integrity	compassion	harmony	unity in diversity	global justice	
aspiration	affinity	love	gender equality	collective security	
reverence for all life	nonviolence	economic equity			
the value of multiculturalism	racial harmony	universal human rights			
WHOLENESS inclusivity	interfaith collaboration	consciousness of world citizenship	world unity		
altruism	philanthropy	(a wider loyalty)	global harmony		
universal education	ecological stewardship		... *the oneness of humanity*		

Reality as a continuum gives a clear evolutionary path to the direction of life. Experiencing the duality side of reality makes us more socially, psychologically, and spiritually ready to turn our consciousness away from the segregated perspective of duality, and move wholeheartedly in the direction toward oneness and unity. Having known duality, we are ready to traverse the principle-centered, value-based side of the continuum in order to realize the fullness of our inherent connectedness as one species, in harmony with all other creatures we share this planet with.

Uniting the One and the Many

The mystery carried within the law of opposition is that the two exist to be made one. Thesis and antithesis (polar opposites) signal a process waiting to be completed; when they are allowed to flow into each other they will create a new and more perfect wholeness. Their synthesis is the goal.

All the world's religious traditions also have the goal of transcending duality and achieving oneness. The Hindu notion of yoga contains the sought-for unity and wholeness that comes with the state of detachment from objects called *nirdvandva*, or being "free from opposites." Buddhists seeking *sadhana* want to realize the paradox expressed in the union of opposites, or the state of nonduality. The Chinese concept of the Tao represents "the way" or method used to unite what is divided.

From the Greeks we inherited a natural theology that recognized all things as derived from one original (divine) source. This is the etymological core of religion: to bind humanity (a part of the many) with its Creator (the One).

The mainstream Judeo-Christian tradition is built upon the human condition resulting from the "fall," or paradise lost, our separation from a state of divine wholeness, and is directed toward recovering this lost unity, as in the prayer of Jesus to his Heavenly Father on behalf of his followers, "...that they may be one as we are one – I in them and you in me – so that they may be brought to complete unity" (John 17: 20-23). Islam, too, has its tradition of transcending duality, especially in the concept of *tawhid*, or divine unity.

The direction of life is from duality to unity. In the mystic treatise *The Seven Valleys*, Baha'u'llah traces the journey of the soul through the valleys of search, love, and knowledge, the planes of limitation in the world of opposites. But the next valley, unity, is a bridge between the temporal and the eternal realm as "the veils of plurality" are pierced and "the heaven of singleness" is entered. There, "the wrappings of illusion" are stripped away and "the lights of oneness" are manifest.

In the valley of unity, we understand the meaning of the Hadith of Muhammad: "Knowledge is a single point, but the ignorant have multiplied it." This consciousness resolves the seeming paradox in the planes of limitation that duality is real, while in the last three valleys (contentment, wonderment, and absolute poverty and true nothingness) "oneness" is the only reality.

Guiding us toward this consciousness of oneness are the revelations of the prophets, each one part of our common spiritual heritage, at the core of which is a universal moral standard of treating others with kindness and genuine mutual respect. Confirming the spark of Divinity within us all, this is what binds us to all of creation.

As centuries pass, our consciousness evolves; we recognize that "love thy neighbor" has its natural extension in "love your enemies." The circle of love keeps expanding, until it becomes unconditional, taking in all: "Vanquish an angry man by gentleness; and overcome the evil man by goodness" (Hinduism); "Full of love for all things in the world, practicing virtue in order to benefit others, this man alone is happy" (Buddhism); "Determine that if people do you good, you will do good to them; and if they oppress you, you will not oppress them" (Islam).

This potential for unconditional love indicates that animosities and conflicts are lingering signs of a limited consciousness. If the present state of affairs appears dark, the not-so-distant future is bright. As Baha'u'llah has predicted, "The whole earth is now in a state of pregnancy. The day is approaching when it will have yielded its noblest fruits…the most enchanting blossoms, the most heavenly blessings."

The spiritual forces guiding us toward oneness are coming into sharper focus, as is the Divine purpose leading us into an uncharted future. With unconditional love as the foundation for a universal code of ethics to build upon, it becomes more realistic to imagine that a great Golden Age of humanity is being ushered in.

Many of the world's leading secular thinkers are now aligned with the world's wisdom traditions as well, sharing the perspective that a single transcendental truth underlies all of reality. "The perennial philosophy" or "the great chain of being" says this can be realized when dualistic consciousness is unified. In Chief Seattle's penetrating words, "All things are connected like to blood that connects us all."

Ervin Laszlo calls this unified view of Reality "The Connectivity Hypothesis." Having evolved from ancient philosophy and on to Einstein, Jung, Sheldrake, and many current quantum theorists, he picks up this thread and brings together all the strands into a single grand unified model, explaining how universal forces of nature interact in harmony with the energy fields of space and the cosmos. "Absolute Reality," he says, is the ultimate expression of the reality of unity.

Lynne McTaggart's *The Field* also points to a unifying concept of the universe. A story told in installments, science has for three centuries, from Newton to Darwin, defined us in terms of our separateness. Now, the latest chapter, written by a group of relatively unknown explorers at the edge of scientific frontiers, "suggests that at our essence we exist as a unity, a relationship—utterly interdependent, the parts affecting the whole at every moment." The implications of this new story are extraordinary.

Physicist Paul Davies, in *The Cosmic Blueprint*, also notes that there is now a "new paradigm of the creative universe, which recognizes the progressive, innovative character of physical processes." It "emphasizes the collective, cooperative and organizational aspects of nature; its perspective is synthetic and holistic rather than analytic and reductionist."

Reality as one also means, according to Deepak Chopra, that even though we can "see eternity in every direction… we choose to cut it into bits and pieces of time and space… [However,] unity is a state in which nothing is left out of 'I am.'"

Or, as Brother Wayne Teasdale put it, "This unity is the heart of all mysticisms. It is awareness of non-duality and non-separation, of no distance between ourselves, the ultimate mystery, and all other beings. The unitive level of consciousness is both integration with the divine and nondual awareness or perception."

The concept of one reality is also practical. Knowing that our life is part of every other life, connected to all living things, means that we have no need to create opposition, conquer, or destroy. This is played out every day in traditional African communities where the value of "*Ubuntu*" still lives in people's hearts. As Archbishop Desmond Tutu explains, Ubuntu "means to know that you are bound up with others in the bundle of life," or that "my humanity is caught up and is inextricably bound up in yours. [Ubuntu] speaks about wholeness...compassion."

These far-ranging worldviews (the Perennial Philosophy, the Great Chain of Being, the Connectivity Hypothesis) all parallel scientific and spiritual ways of describing Ultimate Reality, or God, as "One," a "unified field," "progressive," "collective, cooperative, and organizational," "holistic," with a "purpose," "a metaphysical designer," a "creative power," and "the one and only." These only add to the myriad names of the one Creator already permeating the world's religions.

Consciousness is a unified field, all separation is an illusion, and the diversity that characterizes all life is part of a single unifying force organizing the universe. This force is purposeful and directional in its continuous creative power, and is forever unfolding in a creative, rhythmic, and purposeful way and direction.

A Global Transformation of Consciousness is Under Way

As complexities increase, so do conflicts. In the past century, humanity has experienced more struggle *and* change *and* growth than ever before in its history. Opposing forces have never been so strong, so evident, and so persistent in bringing about progress. The increase of crises, man-made and natural, seems to bring their stamp of doom. Yet, emerging out of this turmoil, humanity has never known a greater, more insatiable appetite for knowledge of all things spiritual and religious.

Historical forces are steadily gathering momentum. The view that material existence represents ultimate reality is waning; economic prosperity at the expense of all else is no longer seen as the primary hallmark of progress, as it once was.

The most formidable force of change now spreading throughout the world is global integration. Rapid and pervasive advances in communication technologies have opened new avenues of interaction among the world's diverse populations; mass travel encircles the globe; profound chosen and forced migrations of enormous numbers of the peoples of all continents have resulted in the intermingling of the world's cultures as citizens of a single homeland; and all these circumstances of the past century have had an unprecedented transformative impact on global consciousness.

We are becoming the recipients of "a new eye, a new ear, a new heart, and a new mind." Yet these are the gifts of an ancient pattern of regular renewal that has occurred throughout history and has been experienced by all those of prior ages who have sought to understand reality.

We live in a time that was longed for by those who lived before us. We are transitioning into our long awaited stage of maturity. We have reached that crucial turning point at which we now sense ourselves as members of one global community.

With each technological advance from the smartphone to the iPad, every terrorist attack from 9/11 to Paris and Istanbul, and every natural disaster from New Orleans to Japan, we are becoming more and more conscious of ourselves as one interconnected world community. Global consciousness characterizes our time in a way never before possible. We have evolved into what we can no longer deny we are—one species. Like birds of one flock, and cells of one body, our individuality is being transformed into our greater interdependence.

It is now within the reach of every human being alive today to cultivate a global consciousness. No longer is it an anomaly to make the whole the priority rather than any of its parts, or to break out of a nationalistic mindset and see the entire world as a whole. Our primary identity can be seen as any one of our smaller group affiliations *or* as the one wider identity that includes all the others. It is now a matter of conscious choice, just as is how far we want to extend and expand our consciousness.

A century and a half ago, the New England Transcendentalists knew from the ancient Upanishads that, as Emerson put it, "There is one mind common to all individual men." Emerson's "Over-soul" described "that Unity... within which every particular man's being is contained and made one with all other..." And thus were the seeds for the interfaith age planted.

In his most recent book, *One Mind*, Larry Dossey takes his place upon the shoulders of Emerson, having been deeply influenced by him as a teenager, and adds to the evolving discussion: "The ethical implications of our fundamental connectedness are profound. Because of our intrinsic oneness, health can never be merely personal, and neither can illness, poverty, or hunger. The unity we share requires a recalibration of the Golden Rule from "Do unto others as you would have them do unto you," to "Be kind to others because in some sense they are you."

The emerging global consciousness engenders a sense of world citizenship, which expresses a love for humanity as a whole. World citizenship is a mindset in which we live with the consciousness to think *and* act globally.

Taking on the identity of a world citizen is adopting a unifying set of values that: a) accepts the interconnectedness of the nations and peoples of the world; b) insists upon a wider loyalty, a love of humanity as a whole; c) commits to a global ethic promoting equitable and sustainable development; d) recognizes humanity as the primary reference group, rather than any one ethnic, social, or nationality group; and, e) considers all lands and countries as home, and all people of each ethnicity, religion, and nation as family.

This vantage point results in a holistic sense of responsibility for protecting individual rights as well as the fate of the planet and the entire human family. Winona LaDuke, Native activist, captures well this sentiment: "We are a part of everything that is beneath us, above us, and around us."

This recognition and the acceptance of the oneness of humanity is sustained by the unifying vision of a peaceful, prosperous world society in which social justice and universal human rights are upheld as the primary values. Education toward this understanding has been the missing dimension of the process. The increased intermingling of the peoples of the world requires comprehensive educational efforts to promote this universal respect, harmony, and unity between all people. Each new level of consciousness brings more awareness of our personal and collective destiny. With our transforming shift underway, we seek to build unity on the grandest scale.

Beyond Political Peace, World Unity is the Goal

Unity defines both the nature of who we are as individual human beings and what we are made for as humanity. World unity is what we are evolving toward. The strongest spiritual force of our time is unity. The power of love has forever been the one driving force directing the ebb and flow and overall advancement of civilization. In our time, the influence of unity and love are the greatest they have ever been.

The body of humanity calls out for its soul. Unity on the grandest scale is the divine remedy and the mightiest instrument for the healing of the world. Unity is more than a mere sense of common purpose, or mutual goodwill. Unity is the force most characteristic of the creative power of the Creator; it is the primary influence driving the progress of civilization, its moral codes, its social and political institutions, its artistic works, technological achievements, and material prosperity. Unity is the power through which humanity's lofty goals will be progressively realized.

It's opposite – disunity – cripples society's progress, and is a fundamental cause of the world's ills. In the midst of our collective ill-ness, it may appear that the collective will or urge to change anything is missing. But unity is a condition of the human spirit. It is in our DNA. It is the very nature of who and what we are.

Unity is not uniformity or sameness. Unity is harmony with difference. Unity can co-exist with difference. Diversity is a fact of life, and always will be. The goal is unity in diversity, or unity with the diversity that exists everywhere. The principle of unity in diversity seeks to broaden the base of society and remold its underlying values and its institutions to keep up with the needs of an ever-changing world.

The flowers of a garden are diverse in color, shape and form, yet are nourished by the waters of one spring and the rays of one sun. They owe their beauty and charm to their diversity. As a rainbow of hues enriches the garden, so does diversity of thought, temperament, and character in the human family.

Human consciousness operates through an infinite variety of individual minds, yet this in no way detracts from its essential unity. Nowhere but in the human body itself, made up of a vast and varied array of organs, tissue structures, bones, systems, and functions, can a more remarkable – and inspiring – example of unity in diversity be found. Unity implies well-being and a coming together.

Unity is central to the evolutionary process, yet its fulfillment depends ultimately upon what is going on inside our own minds, as Teilhard de Chardin notes, "Unity grows... only if it is supported by an increase of consciousness, of vision."

Sharing the Baha'i vision prior to World War II, Shoghi Effendi wrote, "World unity is the hallmark of the stage which human society is now approaching...the goal towards which a harassed humanity is striving. Nation-building has come to an end...A world, growing to maturity, must recognize the oneness and wholeness of human relationships, and establish once and for all the machinery that can best incarnate this fundamental principle of its life."

Writers from many disciplines recognize this emerging unity, too. Historian Arnold Toynbee, who said "The ultimate work of civilization is the unfolding of ever-deeper spiritual understanding," recalls mythologist Joseph Campbell's vision, quoted in this book's introduction: "the unity of the race of man, not only in its biology but also in its spiritual history, which has everywhere unfolded in the manner of a single symphony."

This collective unity was recognized by pioneering quantum physicists, too, who discovered a century ago that there is no separation between physical or spiritual bodies, or among any objects in the universe. As David Bohm said, "Deep down the consciousness of mankind is one," or as Einstein put it, "The field is the only reality."

The progress we've made in less than a century of our transformational journey from a mindset of separate, competing nations, each with its own local interests, to the recognition of our interconnectedness as a global community, with the good of the whole gaining momentum as our necessary common priority, is quite substantial.

This perspective has been echoed in the chambers of the United Nations since its inception by a range of non-governmental organizations, and was recently a focus of a series of international gatherings called by the United Nations to mark the end of one millennium and the beginning of another.

In May 2000, the statement invited by UN Secretary-General Kofi Annan and submitted by over one thousand NGOs made the commitment that: "...We are one human family, in all our diversity, living on one common homeland and sharing a just, sustainable and peaceful world, guided by universal principles of democracy..."

In September of the same year, the Millennium Summit Resolution presented to the UN General Assembly and 149 heads of state and government, reaffirmed "...that the United Nations is the indispensable common house of the entire human family, through which we will seek to realize our universal aspirations for peace, cooperation and development. We therefore pledge our unstinting support for these common objectives, and our determination to achieve them."

As if following an archetypal script, a year later forces opposing this goal reared their head in angry defiance, attacking the World Trade Center only blocks away, unwittingly adding to the resolve of those desiring to achieve such a lofty universal ideal, while most likely unknowingly also contributing to a transformational process already under way. Distinctions between the opposing forces of our time were made sharper, and the crisis the world is experiencing was accelerated all the more. Serious concerns for our collective future are well founded. Yet staying focused on the big picture, we can see a purposeful process gaining momentum.

Except for extremist misconceptions, the forces of history have slowly but consistently been moving us toward the promise of a universal civilization in harmony with itself. Religion cannot be ignored as a force when considering humanity's further development. It represents the most potent positive social force within which the possibilities for the construction of a just and equitable world society are embedded.

All of this progress and regress has followed upon Baha'u'llah's mid 19th-century Revelation, which proclaimed, "The well-being of mankind, its peace and security, are unattainable unless and until its unity is firmly established."

Peace is seen as not only possible but also inevitable in the Baha'i writings for many reasons. Throughout history, the great religions have been the primary agents of the spiritual development of humanity, both individually and collectively. No other force has led people to greater heights of discipline, devotion, and altruistic sacrifice. The human spirit has long been endowed with the capacity to build a balanced material and spiritual civilization.

Now, with a new set of spiritual principles revealed for our time, foremost of which is the unity of the human race, supported further by other social justice principles, we have even greater spiritual capacity. But before peace can be realized, the prerequisite is fully adopting, implementing, and putting into action these spiritual principles that will bring about world unity, which is itself the final prerequisite to world peace. Only this will enable us to finally achieve the balance needed to overcome the long-term devastations of racism, nationalism, and the many social and economic injustices manifest in our world.

Most important, while the fullest capacity and means are there, it is only the deep commitment and conscious choice to act upon this knowledge—which comes with the responsibility of maturity—that will bring this reality into being. If we act accordingly, the fruits of our labors will be realized, as world unity followed by world peace is the next stage in the evolution of the planet.

> *A mind distracted by the many cannot apprehend the One…*
>
> *To go up alone into the mountain and come back as an ambassador to the world has ever been the method of humanity's best friends.*
>
> ~Evelyn Underhill

The ultimate outcome is inevitable; how and when we get there is not. Baha'u'llah calls upon humanity to "be anxiously concerned with the needs of the age ye live in, and center your deliberations on its exigencies and requirements."

Why, then, is humanity's immensely rich spiritual heritage not acknowledged more widely in our ongoing search for truth, harmony, and peace, especially during these trying times? It can no longer be denied or ignored that ours is a time characterized by an intense struggle between the disintegrating dualistic paradigm and the emerging holistic paradigm. We live in an extremely pivotal moment.

Transformative energies are gathering across the planet. Yet few have any real notion of their origin or intended affect. In the next chapter, we shall see how these universal and underlying spiritual principles are guiding our evolution toward maturity and why the realization of our oneness is more evident now than ever before.

Principle 6

Revelation is continuous and progressive

A holistic view of creation shows there has never been a time when humanity has been without a connection to and guidance from the Creator. A consciousness of this interconnectedness has been evident in a continuous line of spiritual teachers, shamans, visionaries, and prophets throughout our long evolution. The release of spiritual energies, essential in our past and future alike, is always needed to transform human hearts, shape new social institutions, and expand circles of unity.

Through such means, our consciousness evolves and our individual and collective development unfolds over time. Today, with our capacity to think globally first, before any other more limited perspective, our global consciousness marks the latest and highest stage in the evolution of our collective life on this planet.

Divine guidance, coming to humanity through the timely appearance of inspired prophets bearing a new Revelation, is progressive and never-ending, the ultimate source of inspiration for both the advancement of consciousness and an ever-advancing civilization. In our time, having been guided to a consciousness of the oneness of humanity, we are prepared to realize our collective coming of age.

6

The Mystery of Divinity

*We spend our lives trying to unlock the mystery of the universe,
but there was a Turkish prisoner who had the key.*

-Leo Tolstoy

*The organization of God is one; the evolution of existence is one; the divine
system is one. Whether they be small or great beings, all are subject to one law
and system.*

-Abdu'l-Baha

*"Moses said to God, 'Suppose I go to the Israelites and say to them 'The God
of your fathers has sent me to you,' and they ask me, 'What is his name?' Then
what shall I tell them? God said to Moses, 'I am that I am. This is what you are
to say to the Israelites: I am sent me to you."'*

-*The Torah*

The quest to understand the greatest mystery of all – the nature of
Divinity – is the religious quest. Religion addresses humanity's ultimate
concerns, the meaning of life, and the very purpose of life. Our pursuit of
these mysteries led us to a clearer sense of what matters most to us, and what

is personally and collectively sacred to us.

This search for transcendent meaning is what most characterizes us as the species *Homo sapiens*. Our ongoing and increasing fascination with the ultimate power and greatest good that we think of as Divinity, or the Creator of all things, has led us to understand that such an infinite, limitless reality can in no way be fully known.

This is a central theme of the 19th-century prophet who Tolstoy referred to as "a Turkish prisoner who had the key." Comprehending the nature of this supreme force is beyond the scope of our finite conceptions or experiences, as Bahá'u'lláh explained: "The Divine Being" always has and will be hidden "in the impenetrable mystery of His unknowable Essence..." This mystery will always remain; the unknown will always surround us. More and more, scientists and other deep thinkers alike acknowledge that our most concerted explorations inevitably lead to yet greater mysteries.

A Holistic View of the Creator

Just as we evolve along the consciousness continuum from self-centeredness to reality-centeredness, or from a focus on the self to a love of humanity, so religion itself is not fixed but rather an evolving series of interconnected cumulative traditions that have undergone change in both structure and form while moving through history. The religion we live by exists within the ever-changing transitory realm of this physical plane, yet has its origin in the one changeless and eternal Source.

As diverse streams representing and defining various approaches to a spiritual life, yet all flowing from the same Creator, each religion has the same connection and "openness to the Divine," offering the seeker of truth a slightly socially determined variation on universal truth. Each has its own practices assisting the common process of transformation, with each leading to liberation from a dependence on the transitory to an enlightenment recognizing the unity of the whole.

The oneness of Divinity becomes more recognizable as the process of ongoing Revelation is visualized as the unfolding, ever-growing tree of religion. From this single living tree has flourished the "Abrahamic" branches, the "Dharmic" branches, and the Indigenous traditions branches.

The Indigenous branches consist of all the ancient and modern Native spiritual traditions throughout the world. They understand this tree as sacred, put here by the Creator of all things, the Great Mystery. It symbolizes unity, connectedness, and eternity, and is believed to be the tree that will gradually gather all the people of the earth under it, as in the Lakota tradition of *The Story of the Sacred Tree.*

From earliest times, spiritual beings, or messengers, have given sacred instructions for sustainable living to peoples of all the Nations. Usually remembered only as the Ancient Ones, a notable exception is The Peacemaker who brought principles of peace, equity, justice, and unity to the warring Nations of upstate New York, unifying them into the Six Nations.

The primary principles of Native spirituality include: the interconnectedness of all Creation; all life is equal; all actions are taken for their long-term effect on all life; and, a thankfulness to the Creator is part of all thought and action. This Indigenous worldview is further characterized by the understanding that although the Creator is not visible anywhere, He is seen everywhere, as Black Elk's thought: "All things are the works of the Great Spirit...He is within all things."

The Abrahamic branches are made up of the line of prophets, or founders of religions, whose direct lineage is traced back to Abraham. This line includes Moses (through Isaac), Jesus (through Isaac), Muhammad (through Ishmael), and Baha'u'llah (through Sarah and Keturah). Each of the religions of these Prophets share the common belief that the Creator guides humanity through revealed teachings to the prophets up to and including those in their own scripture.

The Dharmic branches consist of the religions of the Prophets Krishna, Buddha, and Zoroaster, as well as others originating on the Indian subcontinent, including Jainism and Sikhism. These traditions share certain key concepts such as various forms or interpretations of karma, dharma, samsara, moksha, and yoga.

Visualizing religion as a single tree, Divinity is recognized as the single source of religion. The ancient and ongoing knowledge system of religion itself becomes characterized as an organic process of growth. Having grown for thousands of years, this tree, as with all of nature, has its own seasons of decay and renewal, with new shoots, branches, and leaves, while all its growth is always still part of the same tree.

Many scientists, philosophers, and social scientists also visualize religion as a tree of many branches, periodically renewed by one source. Religion expresses many differences, but there are many more ways in which it is similar. As Abdu'l-Baha expressed it, "Reality is not multiple; it is one. Therefore, the foundations of the religious systems are one because they all proceed from the indivisible reality."

Re-Visioning Religion

There are two ways we can view religion: as consisting of multiple, separate, and independent entities; or, as one evolving knowledge system with many branches. If we view reality as a whole, we also have to see Divine truth as relative, progressive, and unfolding gradually, all the while coming from the same Source. Truth is not known and fixed for all time, but is rather revealed little by little. When more is needed, more follows. If reality is one, truth has to be one.

A long-standing paradox in the comparative study of religions has been: How could there be one Creator and so many religions? This question has perplexed the keenest minds for centuries. Yet, the Messengers of the one Creator have each accepted the prophets before and acknowledged that there would be others to follow.

The continuing nature of divine Revelation has been expressed by Krishna, a principal founder of Hinduism, as: "Whenever dharma declines and the purpose of life is forgotten, I manifest myself on earth. I am born in every age to protect the good, to destroy evil, and to reestablish dharma." In the Bible is written, "And thou shalt be called by a new name, which the mouth of the Lord shall name."

Buddha taught that Brahman is continually manifested in the world: "I am not the first Buddha who came upon earth, nor shall I be the last. In due time another Buddha will arise in the world, a Holy One, a supremely enlightened One... He will reveal to you the same eternal truths... such as I now proclaim."

Christ also took an eternal perspective on the progressive nature of revelation: "I have many things to tell you, but ye cannot bear them now... when the Spirit of truth is come, he will guide you into all truth...and he will show you things to come." Muhammad also looked ahead to the "day unto which mankind shall be gathered together" as "a time appointed," adding, "To each age its Book."

As earlier prophets did for their time, Baha'u'llah, in this age, fulfilled the promises of previous Revelations, reaffirming the progressive nature of religion. In *The Book of Certitude*, Baha'u'llah tells the story of the prophets from Abraham, the "Friend of God," to Moses, "He Who held converse with God," to "the Manifestation of Jesus," and to "the Day-star of Muhammad." They, and the other major prophets (including Krishna, Zoroaster, and Buddha), are all "Treasuries of divine knowledge," each a clearly polished mirror reflecting the light of one sun, each central to the Creator's promise to never leave humanity alone.

The paradox of many religions and one Creator can now be seen holistically. No longer do we need to see the world's religions as separated from each other; rather, they can

> *Men's minds perceive second causes, but only prophets perceive the action of the First Cause.*
> ~Rumi

be seen as joined in purpose and origin. The story of the prophets is the story of the Creator sending a never-ending message to humanity, piece by piece.

In these trying times, we cannot afford to lose sight of the many individual and social benefits humanity has reaped from religion. Within the world's religious and spiritual traditions lie the seeds for rebuilding a tired and worn world.

However, misconceptions still linger about the nature of religion and the way the Creator interacts with an ever-evolving creation; these need to be addressed in public and interfaith discourse in order to ensure the progress of humanity.

Religion needs to be re-envisioned as built upon a dynamic, interconnected sequence of divine Messengers who manifest the attributes of an inaccessible Divinity and convey divinely-inspired Revelations that guide and educate humanity from age to age. As Abdu'l-Baha has put it, "Religion is the outer expression of divine reality. Therefore, it must be living, vitalized, moving, and progressive."

With this perspective, we can see that the founders of the world's major religions (including Abraham, Krishna, Zoroaster, Buddha, Jesus, Muhammad, and Baha'u'llah) each brought messages representing a stage in the limitless unfolding of a single reality which has gradually yet purposively awakened humanity to our true nature, empowered us to serve the evolutionary process itself, and made us the first example of "evolution become conscious of itself," as Huxley noted.

As one universal law governs the entire creation, the same law governs the evolution of religion. How different would our sense of meaning and purpose in life be if we actually saw religion as part of evolution?

It wasn't until the mid-19th century, with the work of Darwin, that evolution even entered popular discourse. We now understand that everything evolves: life, society, cultures, civilization, and especially science and technology. Teilhard de Chardin indicates that evolution itself may be tied to the greatest force of all: "Is evolution a theory, a system or a hypothesis? It is much more: it is a general condition to which all theories, all hypotheses, all systems must bow and which they must satisfy henceforward if they are to be thinkable and true. Evolution is a light illuminating all facts, a curve that all lines must follow."

About the only area of human consciousness we haven't yet accepted as evolving is humanity's relationship to the Creator, or religion itself. The idea that all religions could be seen as pieces of the same puzzle, or the same evolutionary whole, is missing from leading definitions of religion; this idea might even be seen as disrespect for religion itself. Prevailing views of religion try to keep the branches separate from the trunk of the tree they have emerged from.

Re-visioning religion for our time would mean recognizing religion as one, just as we see science as one, though both science and religion have their many branches. Rather than religions having popped up here and there, now and then, at the deepest level religion is religion, as science is science.

Religion has taught us how to love on greater and greater levels over time. The Baha'i writings say, "The purpose of the successive revelations of God is the awakening of humankind to its capacities and responsibilities as the trustee of creation." This process rests upon the progressive unfolding of a single reality.

Baha'u'llah, in his 19th-century revelation, continuing from where the revelation of Muhammad left off some twelve centuries earlier, extended, expanded, and renewed our understanding of ethics, values, and spiritual relativity. He also recast religion as one evolutionary process, one system of knowledge, and as the most compelling force guiding the unfolding of consciousness. He identified the oneness of humanity as the primary spiritual principle of our time; one people occupying one planet. This could not have been envisioned in any of the previous revelations.

Referring to his own revelation and all those preceding and following, Baha'u'llah said, "This is the changeless faith of God, eternal in the past, eternal in the future." This concept, crucial to understanding the evolution of religion, is eloquently, yet mysteriously, expressed in the Gospel of John (1:1-10), "In the beginning was the Word... and the Word was God... There was a man sent from God... He was not that Light, but he was sent to bear witness of that Light. He was in the world, and the world was made by him."

The Missing Chapter in the Story of Religion

To think that divine revelation could be sealed, or would suddenly come to an end at some point, is to misunderstand a boundless, omnipotent Creative power that continually, within its own rhythm, reveals portions of its grand design.

A new chapter begins in the ever-evolving story of religion each time a messenger of the Creator appears. A community of believers forms around this renewed source of spiritual life, consciousness is shifted, and all aspects of individual and social life move forward. The arts and sciences are revivified, the legal system and goals of social affairs are restructured, and a new civilization emerges and begins to transform the efforts and capacities of human beings in all regions of the world.

Throughout the centuries that follow, society more readily recognizes the transforming power that has caused a leap in its own consciousness. Continuing to draw from the release of spiritual energies, the patterned cycle runs its natural course.

In a few millennia, with each new revelation, humanity has seen its unity expand successively, from family to tribe to cities and then on to nations. Now, just in time to help usher in the much-needed next stage of world unity, we are witness to an emerging global consciousness, initiated by the release of a new revelation.

The revelation of Baha'u'llah begins the cycle again, and for the first time the effects of the release of these spiritual energies have been visible on a truly global scale only a century later. Recent 20th and early 21st century world shattering events (genocide, world wars, and unprecedented numbers of refugees worldwide) are the first stages of the universal transformation of society set in motion by this infusion, speeding up of the breakdown of the old needed to bring about a rebirth and renewal.

Reaffirming the message in the Gospel of John that has fascinated readers for two millennia, Baha'u'llah wrote of his own Revelation: "No sooner had the First Word proceeded out of His mouth ... than the whole creation was revolutionized, and all that are in the heavens and all that are on earth were stirred to the depths. Through that Word the realities of all created things were shaken, were divided, separated, scattered, combined and reunited, disclosing... entities of a new creation, and revealing... the signs and tokens of Thy unity and oneness."

The Prophets of God have always been essential to this process. Deepak Chopra has described the universe as a "reality sandwich," with the top layer being "God," the bottom layer being the "material world," where we reside, and the middle layer being the "transition zone," where "God and humans meet on common ground." The transition zone is a bridge between the other two layers, uniting them with such things as miracles, visions, and enlightenment, or experiences of Divine presence.

The all-important "transition zone" is further enhanced in the Baha'i writings as being where the world of the prophets exists to bridge the world of God and the world of humanity. As the Creator's intermediaries, the prophets link the world of Divinity and the world of humanity by bringing teachings, releasing spiritual energies, and helping to facilitate such experiences of connection with the Divine.

This new "filling" of the reality sandwich, a long line of prophets bringing a new spiritual feast to each age, creates an image of three parallel horizontal lines, representing the worlds of God, the prophets, and humanity, completed by a vertical line also representing the prophets, who bridge the upper and lower layers, creating the common ground between them, and uniting them.

Referring to these layers of reality, the Prophets of God, the religions they have founded, and how they all fit together, Baha'u'llah has said, "These principles and laws, these firmly-established and mighty systems, have proceeded from one Source and are the rays of one Light. That they differ one from another is to be attributed to the varying requirements of the ages in which they were promulgated."

But a Divine revelation is more than just words, teachings, or even a holy book. By its very nature, each Revelation releases a pervasive spiritual energy, power, or force that, though latent until activated by human endeavors, opens the hearts and minds of artists, scientists, and others, transforming individuals and civilization alike.

These spiritual forces are patterned energy, a configuration of society-building forms that hold everything in order, regulate the world of humanity, and instill into the entire human race the capacity to achieve its destined oneness, unity, and peace.

Throughout history, the prophets have always had the primary objective of preparing human consciousness, by stages, to gradually recognize the oneness of humanity. Each era has initiated a progressive leap of consciousness toward this, yet there is no essential difference between any of the Divine Revelations, except in the changing needs of the age in which they appear.

This spiritual principle is summed up by sociologist Nader Saiedi as follows: "The doctrine of progressive revelation explains the unveiling of the divine in the realm of human history as itself a historical process: religion both interacts with society yet is not reducible to a social construction. All the religions have one and the same source, and divine revelation renews itself perpetually in accordance with divine purpose. Divine revelation is not a static, absolute, and unique event; and spiritual journey is a feature not only of individuals but also of humanity as a collectivity."

Also explaining this unity of the prophets, Shoghi Effendi, the Guardian of the Baha'i Faith, wrote in a 1947 statement prepared for the United Nations:

"The fundamental principle enunciated by Baha'u'llah... is that religious truth is not absolute but relative, that Divine Revelation is a continuous and progressive process, that all the great religions of the world are divine in origin, that their basic principles are in complete harmony, that their aims and purposes are one and the same, that their teachings are but facets of one truth, that their functions are complementary, that they differ only in the nonessential aspects of their doctrines, and that their missions represent successive stages in the spiritual evolution of human society..."

This sequential revealing of one continuous spiritual truth points to the common origin of the world's religions *and* the successive stages in social evolution. The primary focus of each Revelation has progressed from the individual level (the Revelation of Christ) to the national (the Revelation of Muhammad) and to the global level (the Revelation of Baha'u'llah). This has added wider and more inclusive levels to divine guidance as human needs expanded and became more complex collectively.

While the Gospels focused on providing spiritual guidance for the individual to attain a high moral standard, six centuries later, the Qur'an introduced the concept of the nation as a unit and a vital stage in the evolution of human society ("Love of one's country is an element of the Faith of God"). In addition to an individual code of ethics, the principle of nationhood was also required at that time.

By the mid-nineteenth century, as social evolution approached its stage of maturity, the need emerged for the Revelation of Baha'u'llah to identify the principle of "the consciousness of the oneness of mankind" as its "distinguishing feature" and "central theme." Now, the unity of humankind can not only be envisioned but also achieved, as the seven continents of the earth have become a global village.

This evolutionary perspective on the unfolding of religion explains the vast changes and differences that have occurred from one spiritual epoch to another. It enables us to see that the diversity of religious customs, practice, and even doctrine can be compared to the diversity in dress, healing methods, hygiene, dietary preferences, transportation systems, and economic activity between cultural, ethnic, and nationality groups. In neither case do these examples of human diversity disprove the principle of the oneness of humanity.

Supporting this central theme in the Baha'i writings is a set of spiritual precepts that will make possible a new level of unity in diversity in our time; they make up the foundation of this new paradigm guiding us toward a consciousness of oneness, social justice in all realms, *and* world unity:

1. *The independent investigation of reality is a fundamental obligation of all human beings.* Blindly and uncritically following various traditions, movements, or opinions is still one of the main sources of conflict in the world today. Everyone has the capacity and responsibility to distinguish truth from falsehood; an unfettered search for truth will reveal that truth is one.

2. *True religion is in harmony with reason and the pursuit of scientific knowledge.* A major source of conflict today is the opinion that one must choose between a life of faith or reason. Science and religion are two knowledge systems under the all-encompassing umbrella of one reality. They are mutually reinforcing; both advance civilization. The truths of science are discovered, and the truths of prophetic religion are revealed, both facets of one truth.

3. *Women and men are equal in the sight of their Creator.* The full equality in all fields of endeavor between genders is one of the most important prerequisites for peace. Injustice against half the world's population promotes harmful attitudes and habits among the other half. Feminine values and qualities—such as compassion, nurturance, cooperation and empathy—have to be brought to the forefront of everyone's consciousness.

4. *There is a spiritual solution to the world's economic problems.* The ever-expanding extremes of poverty and wealth cannot continue to widen.

A very small percentage of humanity holds the greatest wealth, while the vast majority live in poverty. In order to achieve balanced global prosperity, all available human and material resources, rather than being used only for the short-term advantage of a few, have to be used for the long-term good of all.

5. *All forms of prejudice – religious, ethnic, national, or class – must be replaced with the recognition of our oneness.* Discrimination, oppression, or racism toward any group causes all of society to suffer, and keeps us from realizing world unity and lasting peace. Only a deeper respect for the intrinsic value of each culture *and* individual will help us see that our diversity is a means for us fulfilling our potential *and* an expression of our wholeness.

6. *The variety of religious expression in the world has the same source and shares a unity of purpose.* Religious truth is not absolute, but relative; its essence is unity and oneness. The continually unfolding message of all the Prophets is one and the same; their spiritual and social teachings are appropriate to their time, and facets of one truth illuminating one reality.

7. *Humanity is one family.* Having passed though the stage of its childhood, humanity is now struggling to leave behind its adolescent ways while taking on new patterns of thought and action in approaching its maturity. Accepting the oneness of humanity as a biological fact, a social necessity, and a spiritual reality will lead us further along our journey toward lasting world peace.

8. *Nature is the embodiment of the Divine.* The whole earth is sacred; its vast resources are a common heritage *and* trust for all humanity, now and into the farthest future. An intricate web of interdependent relationships sustains our planet. Our collective survival depends upon the care and protection of the natural environment – all plant life, animal life, and sea life. Environmental vandalism is caused by

the corruption of the moral fabric that guides and disciplines human life; indeed, climate change is an ethical issue. We must become more conscious of our attitudes and actions towards the source of our sustenance; we must extend our compassion to all living things. With a firm and binding set of environmental ethics, we must answer the call to environmental stewardship of the planet. Ecological health is inextricably tied to spiritual health.

These interrelated precepts regarding gender equality, economic equity, racial unity, scientific and religious harmony, environmental stewardship, and the others outlined above, along with a universal auxiliary language, universal education (with urgent emphasis on girls' education), work performed in the spirit of service, and a global commonwealth built upon principles of collective security, are the revealed truths of our age. They were enunciated by Baha'u'llah in the second half of the 19th century as an all-embracing vision of humanity's future to lead us from a consciousness of duality to a consciousness of oneness.

So interdependently tied together are these precepts that the realization of one depends upon the realization of all the others. They are each aspects of the over-arching principle of the oneness of humanity, whose fate will be determined by the

> *Do not hope that I shall deny my faith, even in appearance for one moment, for an aim so childish as that of conserving for a few more days a transient form which has no value.*
>
> *No, if I am questioned, and I shall be, I shall have the happiness of giving my life for God...*
>
> *You can kill me as soon as you like, but you cannot stop the emancipation of women.*
>
> ~Tahirih (Qurratu'l-'Ayn) (1852)

collective depth of conviction given over to these spiritual precepts of our time.

These eight precepts resonate with the spirit of the age; they are today's equivalent of the Ten Commandments. As these precepts are put into practice, as were earlier scriptural injunctions against idolatry, theft, and false witness in their time, these will be clearly recognized as catalysts to an ever-advancing civilization, and pre-requisites to world unity and lasting peace.

Humanity's Coming of Age

There are still signs of characteristic adolescent turmoil evident all around us. But we are inevitably moving, as a species, into an era of higher-ordered thinking, based on new realities and necessities. There are also signs of development toward understanding greater responsibilities, more engaged collaborations, sustained cooperation, and wider loyalties, all recognizing a collective purpose and direction.

A global ethic is emerging, with its origin in a universal set of values. As the author of *The Clash of Civilizations and the Remaking of World Order* put it, "Whatever the degree to which they divided humankind, the world's major religions – Christianity, Hinduism, Buddhism, Islam, Confucianism, Taoism, Judaism – share key values in common. If humans are ever to develop a universal civilization, it will emerge gradually through the exploration and expansion of these commonalities."

This global ethic is reflected in all these world religions as well as the more recent Baha'i Faith: "The earth is but one country, and mankind its citizens," and "Ye dwell in one world, and have been created through the operation of one Will."

The Parliament of the World's Religions 1993 declaration on a "global ethic" also stated that this "already exists within the religious teachings of the world," and that we are seeing a "new consciousness of ethical responsibility" evident in many areas of life. While they noted that it is the special task of religions to pass these timeless, universal values on to future generations, they concluded, "Earth cannot be changed for the better unless the consciousness of individuals is changed." This is what will lead us to an acceptance of a global ethic built upon the core spiritual principle of our time – the consciousness of the oneness of humanity.

Ultimately, this principle, the building block upon which all the other principles would follow, is a spiritual truth that is becoming more and more evident every day as what is needed to achieve a peaceful, unified world. All the human, social, and natural sciences confirm today that we are but one human species, albeit infinitely varied in the secondary aspects of life.

Leading thinkers today recognize this fundamental principle of the global age. Ervin Laszlo states that mankind "needs a star to follow," or "standards by which we can direct our steps." These will come from "the great ideals of the world religions," he says, from the Christian vision of universal brotherhood, Judaism's vision of all the families of the earth being blessed, Islam's universal vision of an ultimate community of God, man, and nature, the Hindu vision of matter as the outward manifestation of spirit attuned to cosmic harmony, the Buddhist vision of all reality as interdependent, and the Confucian vision of supreme harmony in ordered human relationships.

Laszlo goes on, "The essential goal of the Baha'i Faith is to achieve a vision that is world-embracing and could lead to the unity of mankind and the establishment of a world civilization based on peace and justice." These "are perennial ideals based on universally human values," and need to be rediscovered to guide our steps.

However, Laszlo seems to be relatively alone among leading edge thinkers in recognizing a necessary link in the Great Chain of Being. Humanity's evolution not only appears to be progressive, but so does religion's, he concludes, and with a surprising and insightful twist.

The average person has a linear concept of progress, with conditions improving year after year. Juxtaposed to this, with recent setbacks including the atomic bomb, nuclear disasters, oil spills, and economic downturns, is the opposite image of linear *regress*, a limits-to-growth pessimism culminating in a global catastrophe. But Laszlo says there is now emerging a concept of historical progress that is "less naïve and more realistic than the linear progress or regress concept dominant in public consciousness." He explains:

"Although the scientific concept has been discovered only recently, remarkably enough, its main outlines have been anticipated in the 19th century by a Persian prophet whose influence is only now beginning to be felt in the modern world. Over one hundred years ago, Baha'u'llah, founder of the Baha'i Faith, proclaimed that the oneness of mankind will be achieved in evolutionary stages replete with strife, chaos, and confusion. Historical development begins with the birth of the family, the advent of tribal society, and continues in turn with the constitution of the city-state and other political units. In recent times these units have expanded into independent sovereign nations. The next stage in this social evolution, Baha'u'llah taught, is the organization of human society as a planetary civilization which will be characterized by the emergence of a world community, the consciousness of world citizenship and the founding of a world civilization and culture which would allow for an infinite diversity in the characteristics of its components.

The world state, the consummation of human evolution, will come about through periods of upheaval...Writing in lifelong confinement in the Ottoman prison colony of Acre towards the end of the nineteenth century, Baha'u'llah noted that 'winds of despair' are blowing in every direction. The strife that divides and afflicts the human race is increasing; the signs of impending convulsions can be discerned. A hundred years later his followers, members of the now rapidly growing Baha'i world community, recognize this non-linear evolutionary trend and are committed to acting in accordance with it."

Laszlo connects this divinely inspired revelatory non-linear perspective with the scientific view that emerged in the late twentieth century of systems thinkers like Ludwig von Bertalanffy, Norbert Wiener, and Ilya Prigogine.

Meaningful evolution would not be possible without this confrontation and ultimate union of opposites. Laszlo, therefore, sees no disagreement between science and religion in recognizing a common force guiding evolutionary progress toward a consciousness of oneness. Both emphasize the interconnected nature of all things, as they are all one reality. And both acknowledge an ultimate mystery behind it all.

A new life, a new chapter in humanity's story, is emerging from the decay of yesterday. The springtime of the inner world is infusing a new spirit into the outer world. Unseen but ever-present spiritual forces, revealed progressively and cyclically, are being released in our time, pushing evolution to higher levels of convergence, signaling humanity's coming of age. We live at the conjunction of transformation and integration, where world unity is a realizable goal as we build a culture of oneness, the foundation of a new civilization.

Principle 7

Consciousness evolves toward wholeness and unity

Science and religion agree that consciousness does not reside just in the human brain, but rather pervades the entire universe. As one universal law governs all, the multitude of ways of seeing the universe eventually come together and join in one reality, one organic whole, a grand synthesis.

In a nonrandom universe, there is a plan behind the rose, the hummingbird, the whale, and this shimmering globe drifting in orderly fashion through the heavens. Contemplating the most profound of mysteries, our minds recognize an Intelligence beyond anything we can imagine. This leads our consciousness to new dimensions and understandings, giving us ever-greater glimpses into the wholeness of reality.

Examining them more closely than ever, opposites all around us naturally come to overlap more than ever. Science and religion, as our two primary knowledge systems, are and always have been part of the same whole; they cannot be in opposition to one another. As we approach fulfilling our potential, we witness the Divine in everything, the wholeness and unity hidden beyond all boundaries, and the veils of illusion burn away as a single glance reveals one creation. Evolution has all along been leading us toward concord and harmony, toward an ever-more unified and peaceful civilization.

7

The Inherent Harmony of Reason and Faith

*As man advances in civilization,
and small tribes are united into larger communities, the simplest
reason would tell each individual that he ought to extend his social instincts
and sympathies to all members of the same nation,
though personally unknown to him.*

-Charles Darwin

*More than anything else, the future of civilization
depends on the way the two most powerful forces of
history, science and religion,
settle into relationship with each other.*

-Alfred North Whitehead

*We are explorers and the most compelling frontier of our time
is human consciousness.
Our quest is the integration of science and spirituality,
a vision that reminds us of our connectedness to the inner self, to each other,
and to the Earth.*

-Edgar Mitchell

We have gradually become more aware of an underlying order to the universe. At an earlier time, people thought they were the center of the universe; today we know there are over one hundred billion galaxies. In sync with each other, each divine revelation has opened the floodgates for further scientific discovery. Together, they move us closer to uncovering the mysteries of existence.

But when we persist in compartmentalizing knowledge into separate categories or disciplines we cover up a larger unity. Science and religion, rather than competing with each other, complement each other. Each offers necessary perspectives that advance our consciousness and enable an understanding of the whole that is reality.

Grasping this interdependent relationship of science and religion is key to our survival, as Whitehead notes. They *are* the two most powerful forces of history. Our quest, as Mitchell puts it, is to recognize their integrated relationship; science and religion provide us with the necessary halves of such a balanced whole.

Did Darwin Discover Divinity?

We've seen one example illustrating the interdependence of science and religion in chapter two. A primary virtue revered by all the world's religions is altruism, which also happens to be something science tells us is built into our genes, expressed as the tendency to act with an unselfish regard for others. Putting these two knowledge systems together makes this understanding even more meaningful.

Humans survive—and thrive—in groups that support and protect each other. Altruism is a well-documented human trait, especially present in times of great duress and oppression. It is as strong a trend of evolution, if not stronger, than competition.

This view is championed by biologist/anthropologist David Sloan Wilson in his landmark book, *Does Altruism Exist? Culture, Genes, and the Welfare of Others*, which shows that religious traditions are not alone in recognizing the interconnectedness of all life; in fact, the fields of physics, complex systems thinking, and ecology are approaching the same destination. The scientific conversation that began with Charles Darwin's evolutionary theories has expanded to include every discipline of study.

But what did Darwin really have to say about the curious convergence of a scientific discovery connected to religious virtues? Tucked away in *The Descent of Man* is his recognition that the natural law of cooperation co-exists with the law of the survival of the fittest. In developing his "evolution through natural selection" thesis, he did veer away just enough to speculate on how far the natural law of cooperation might go in the human species. The rest of the quote referred to earlier is:

"As man advances in civilization, and small tribes are united into larger communities, the simplest reason would tell each individual that he ought to extend his social instincts and sympathies to all members of the same nation, though personally unknown to him. This point being once reached, there is only an artificial barrier to prevent his sympathies extending to the men of all nations and races."

Here, Darwin unites his own material law of survival of the fittest with the crowning spiritual law, the Golden Rule, known in all sacred traditions as 'do unto others as you would have them do unto you,' the ethic of reciprocity, or, as expressed by Martin Luther King, Jr., the love ethic.

As his quote shows, Darwin extended the natural law of cooperation from the individual level to the global level. This lays the framework for another universal spiritual principle, a future in which there would be peace on earth, or—as Darwin here envisions—what evolution itself is leading us toward.

In this overlooked reflection, we have what may be Darwin's clearest expression of evolution on the largest scale. Known for examining the minutiae of nature, he offers here an outline of the grandest theme of all.

In this one statement, he seems to have understood human nature as grounded in goodness, with an impulse toward altruism. It seems fair to think that in today's global conditions he would advocate for utilizing the capacities of our reasoning for an ethic that placed compassionate action above the interests of nations.

For all the debate that Darwin's views on evolution have created, his real views may not have been that far from an understanding of the harmony of science and religion, that they are both part of a larger order bringing meaning to creation.

When Darwin wrote, "All the organic beings which have ever lived on this earth have descended from some one primordial form," could he have been thinking that all life is literally made of the same stuff? Could this have actually foreshadowed the discovery almost a century later of DNA, in which every organism carries a code for its own creation in its cells, a common language to all life? Modern Darwinians don't have to guess at the story of evolution; they consult "genetic scripture."

What stronger indication can there be for one common source of all life than all created beings having a common connection in their genetic code? Genetic scripture is a newly discovered code for helping us understand the physical realm, just as religious scripture, revealed by the Prophets of God, has long been the code for guiding us through the spiritual realm. Separately, each reveal parallel aspects of the same reality; together, they give us the bigger picture of the whole.

The discoveries of Darwin and his descendants, though many still shy away from the term, all point to a purposeful universe progressing in a clear direction toward a known goal, perhaps what Einstein called "the rationality of the universe."

It was not that far from the discovery of DNA to geneticist Dean Hamer's direct connection between genes and God. In his bridge-building book, *The God Gene: How Faith is Hardwired into Our Genes*, he asks: Is there a biological basis for spiritual experience? Why is such a transcendental awareness universal among all cultures? He sees spirituality as an innate instinct leading us toward optimism, faith, and meaning.

Darwin's reasoning that our social instincts and sympathies evolve from "small tribes" to "larger communities" to "all members of the same nation" to, finally, "all nations and races" has to be seen as an extension of his principle of evolution through natural selection. This aligns with the spiritual principle of evolution through the progressive unfolding of order toward greater and greater harmony.

Darwin, whose early career led him from medical school to divinity school to HMS *Beagle*, states as much himself, "As natural selection works solely by and for the good of each being, all corporeal and mental endowments will tend to progress toward perfection." His progression "toward perfection" represents as much of a purposeful direction to evolution as anything could.

The release of the Baha'i Revelation, during Darwin's lifetime, could have inspired his view of evolution as progressing "toward perfection," as seen here: "All beings, whether large or small, were created perfect and complete from the first, but their perfections appear in them by degrees… In the seed all perfections exist from the beginning, but appear little by little. The shoot, the branches, leaves, blossoms, and fruits, all these things are in the seed, potentially, though not apparently."

To this is added the further clarification, "The growth and development of all beings is gradual….The seed does not at once become a tree; the embryo does not at once become a man; the mineral does not suddenly become a stone. No, they grow and develop gradually and attain to the limit of perfection. This is the universal divine organization and the natural system."

A Hidden Wholeness Removes The Boundaries

In an intriguing way, Darwin's thinking on progressive evolution and the common origin of all life parallels a core concept of the Perennial Philosophy: everything is connected with everything else, and "as above so below." Examples of this idea range from Shintoism ("Regard Heaven as your father, Earth as your mother, and all things as your brothers and sisters") to Buddhism ("One Reality, all-comprehensive, contains within itself all realities") and to the Lakota ("With all things and in all things, we are relatives"). All agree that the only way to really understand the reality of individual things is in their relationship to the whole.

In contemporary thinking, the concept of everything being connected with everything else is the foundation of the systems view of the world. The approach known as "the grand synthesis" unites physical, biological, and social evolution into a systematic whole, which also unites the knowledge systems of science and religion because they all express the same universal laws, patterns, and principles.

Nor is there anything unusual about the progressive nature of either science *or* religion. They have more similarities than differences, especially in the way knowledge unfolds and advances. Science grows sequentially under the guidance of great teachers such as Aristotle, Ptolemy, Copernicus, Kepler, Galileo, Newton, Einstein – who create a natural progression of evolving thought, each one figuratively standing on the shoulders of the one who preceded him, and thereby seeing farther.

The same is true of the major prophets, *and* they are even less enemies of each other than Copernicus was of Ptolemy. Buddha did not deny Krishna. Nor did Christ oppose Moses; they each declared that they

> The lamps are different but the Light is the same...
> One matter, one energy, one Light, one Light-mind,
> Endlessly emanating all things...
> Ground yourself, strip yourself down,
> To blind loving silence. Stay there, until you see
> You are gazing at the Light with its own ageless eyes.
> ~Jalal ad-Din Rumi

were part of an unfolding system of truth.

Just as the revelation of religious truth is continuous and progressive, so are the discoveries of science. True religion and sound science support one another. The principles of one cannot be in opposition to the other. They are complementary paths to the same reality. Both are needed, just as are two wings to fly. Reason is one wing, faith the other. Science and religion are the yin and yang of reality; both have the same source assisting their unfoldment and the same creation to illuminate. Both have to be in harmony, and both are necessary for us to fully understand reality as a whole.

The unbiased investigation of reality will reveal the interdependence of science and religion. Abdu'l-Baha explains, "If a question be found contrary to reason, faith and belief in it are impossible... Can the heart accept that which reason denies?" Matters of belief need not threaten scientists; matters of reason need not threaten spiritual thinkers.

If we are conscious of science and religion as two halves of a whole, each supporting the other, the boundaries between them become less identifiable until they actually disappear. We will also be able to see then that there is more and more overlap in their realms than ever thought possible.

Einstein is one of the leading scientists who wanted to remove the pseudo-boundaries between these knowledge systems: "Science without religion is lame, religion without science is blind." That is, each needs the other and must make sense, separately and together. Without the other, each is incomplete. And, from both a scientific and spiritual perspective, it was Teilhard de Chardin who predicted in 1924, "Science will, in all probability, be increasingly impregnated by mysticism."

This unified perspective has spawned many books that blend, merge, or integrate science and religion: *God and the Brain*; *The Science of Medical Intuition*; *The Language of God*; *The Mind of the Universe*; *Reinventing the Sacred*; *The Elegant Universe*; *The Physics of Immortality*; and, *The God Theory*. They all seem to understand well what Paul Davies said, "By means of science we see into the mind of God."

Philosophers and spiritual thinkers also link the two systems of knowledge: *From Science to God*; *The Marriage of Sense and Soul*; *Quantum Shift in the Global Brain*; *The Science of Religion*; *The Big Questions in Science and Religion*; *The Biology of Transcendence*; *The Tao of Physics*; and, *Quantum Physics and Theology*. Explorations like these make terms like mystical science and scientific spirituality much more plausible.

A remarkable evolution of consciousness is evident since the mid-19th century. Peter Russell says the common ground shared by both science and religion brings "the two halves of humanity's search for truth together under the same roof." This merging is vital for the deeper understanding it affords, and for our future existence.

This is why we need a new story of consciousness, one that accounts for the recent progressions that have brought us, individually and collectively, to the threshold of the consciousness of oneness.

Religion has always acknowledged the Intelligence that guides the rhythm of the cosmos. And scientists are increasingly noticing the same thing. Quantum physicists, typified by David Bohm's "unbroken wholeness of the cosmos," or the "implicate order," have found that the physical universe holds the keys to the most mystical of realms, that nature is intelligent and purposeful, and that all information about its laws and principles is present but hidden in some higher reality.

Humbled in the face of this mysterious interconnectedness, Max Planck said, "Science can not solve the ultimate mystery of nature. And that is because, in the last analysis, we ourselves are… part of the mystery that we are trying to solve." Einstein, in contemplating the unknown said "The harmony of natural law" revealed "an intelligence of such superiority that, compared with it, all the systematic thinking and acting of human beings is an utterly insignificant reflection."

Each great discovery throughout time has removed another curtain on the window of Creation, giving us a greater glimpse into its marvels. In 1859, Darwin's *The Origin of Species* signaled the beginning of the greatest flood of scientific discoveries humanity has seen, while also making it scientifically accepted that all organisms are connected, or part of "the great Tree of Life."

This was already known by the world's spiritual traditions, and had been confirmed again in the Baha'i revelation, just prior to Darwin's discoveries: "The utterance of God is a lamp, whose light is these words: Ye are the fruits of one tree, and the leaves of one branch." Therefore, the quote goes on, "Deal ye with one another with the utmost love and harmony, with friendliness and fellowship."

Where Darwin had discovered that natural selection is the chief force driving evolutionary change, the Baha'i teachings confirm that there are sacred forces guiding the evolution of the universe itself, and therefore our consciousness of it: "Ye dwell in one world, and have been created through the operation of one Will." And it clarifies the extent and breadth of this Will. "The progress of the world, the development of nations, the tranquility of peoples, and the peace of all who dwell on earth are among the principles and ordinances of God."

Still in the early stages of becoming known to the majority of humanity, this revelation brings religion into the modern age and verifies the latest quantum discoveries: "This endless universe is like the human body… all its parts are connected one with another and are linked together in the utmost perfection."

Indeed, the Baha'i writings from the second half of the 19th century shed remarkable light upon the latest quantum energy field thinking: "All phenomena are realized through the divine bounty…the phenomena of the universe find realization through the one power animating and dominating all things, and all things are but manifestations of its energy and bounty."

We have arrived at the point in time where the story we tell of the creation and its unfolding makes all the difference in the world, as Brian Swimme has noted: "For the first time in human history, we can agree on the basic story of the galaxies, the stars, the planets, minerals, life forms, and human cultures. This story does not diminish the spiritual traditions of the classical or tribal periods of human history. Rather, the story provides the proper setting for the teachings of all traditions, showing the true magnitude of their central truths."

Welcoming the Interfaith, Interspiritual Age

Removing the boundaries between science and religion also softens the boundaries between religions. We are, in fact, entering the interspiritual age, where all things are being understood as interconnected. All the parts of the puzzle are coming together to construct the whole. Social and sacred are merging today like never before, much like a "grand synthesis," an over-arching integration.

Great forces of progress are at work in the world. In only some hundred and seventy years since the beginning of the Darwinian era, we have more information now about a unified field theory of existence than the world had then about evolution.

The pioneers of quantum physics found that "at our essence we exist as a unity, a relationship—utterly interdependent, the parts effecting the whole at every moment." This is the reality the Baha'i revelation identified as the primary principle of this age: the oneness of humanity. Yet, only the hard work needed to achieve basic human rights and the core social justice needs of our age will manifest this unity in the world.

This is still a relatively young global movement that needs to get its footing on firm ground. But it all comes down to how we use our consciousness, whether we use it to connect to the source of all consciousness. The Baha'i writings say the goal of the evolution of human consciousness is that humanity should reflect the perfect unity that already exists in the creation. Because the human mind is finite, but with great potential, we have help in this task from the missing ingredient in the "reality sandwich," the Prophets of God, who guide and inspire all of humanity to a deeper awareness of reality. Their spiritual energies assist us in fulfilling our potentialities.

In this spirit of interconnectedness, and service to the betterment of humanity, a growing network of worldwide interfaith and interspiritual groups, along with social movements are putting into action the much-needed universal principles of our time.

It all began with the globalizing forces making an interfaith movement possible in the mid-1800s. The telegraph, the railroad, the steamship, and many more soon-to- follow paradigm-shifting inventions sped up communication and knit the world together in ways it never had been before.

The world was becoming smaller, and with one Creator with one purpose, these forces can be recognized as all part of the same grand synthesis of our evolutionary process toward the realization of our oneness. The world's religions started moving closer together just like everything else in the world.

Around this same time, the world's sacred scriptures began being translated into other languages, too, opening the way for a new field of study, the study of comparative religion, led by Freeman Clarke's 1871 classic *Ten Great Religions*.

While American Transcendentalists may have been the first to build a bridge between Western and Eastern religions, it was the first Parliament of the World's Religions in 1893 in Chicago, though dominated by American Protestants, that provided the first platform for the direct exchange of thoughts, beliefs, and worldviews between faith communities as widespread as Islam, African American traditions, Buddhism, Eastern Orthodox Christianity, Jainism, Hinduism, Judaism, and Baha'i, thus ushering in the global interfaith movement.

Though it was a century before the next Parliament of the World's Religions, interest in Eastern religions continued to grow on its own and through the founding of the Vedanta Society in 1894. The first formal dialogue among faith communities, though all Christian, started with the creation of the Federal Council of Churches at the beginning of the 20th century, which led to the World Council of Churches. Following this, with a gradual and more general acceptance of other world religions, the World Congress of Faiths came into being in 1936 in London. Protestant-Catholic-Jewish dialogue was becoming more common by mid-century.

In 1960, the Temple of Understanding was created by Juliet Hollister "to draw people together to build a movement embracing all faiths." She had the early support of Eleanor Roosevelt, Albert Schweitzer, Thomas Merton, and many others. Today, it carries out many worldwide programs of interfaith education, sustainability, and justice, all addressing the new challenges of an interconnected, global society.

The Immigration Act of 1965 not only opened America's doors to the entire world, abolishing old quotas based on northern European nationality, it also transformed cultural and religious diversity in America, resulting in the much quicker spreading of Hindu and Buddhist teachings through the influx of the many swamis, gurus, lamas, and roshis that came to America over the next thirty years.

With its growing diversity, the rest of the 60s, 70s, and beyond saw interfaith gatherings and dialogue gradually become somewhat more inclusive, extending in some settings, like universities, to Muslims, Hindus, Buddhists, and sometimes Baha'is.

This was also due in part to the Vatican II declaration of 1966, *Nostra Aetate*, which created the framework for inter-religious relations and dialogue with the Roman Catholic Church, as well as to a continuing general trend to learning about difference and diversity of religious views.

The 1993 Parliament of the World's Religions attracted the most diverse group of people ever to meet in one place in the history of humankind. At that time Chicago was a city with hundreds of Hindu, Buddhist, Zoroastrian, and Jain temples, Sikh gurudwaras, mosques, and a Baha'i House of Worship. This Parliament also gave birth to the Declaration Toward a Global Ethic, an extraordinary interfaith consensus of universal human values that can sustain an interdependent world.

The event itself, according to Brother Wayne Teasdale, was one in which "The divine showed up and opened everyone, inspiring enthusiasm, mutual trust, receptivity, and a wonderful sense of joy... We were not of one mind but of one heart... The spirit gave us a whole new paradigm of relationship in the existential experience of community..."

That same year, United Religions Initiative came into being as a bridge-building organization to promote enduring interfaith cooperation, to end religiously motivated violence, and to create cultures of peace, justice and healing for the Earth and all living beings. Today, it has grown to include over 700 interfaith Cooperation Circles in 85 countries, and is the largest grassroots interfaith network in the world.

In 1999, Wayne Teasdale wrote that we are at the dawn of a new consciousness, a new segment of historical experience, what he called the *Interspiritual Age*. This is a step beyond the interfaith age, because it acknowledges a spiritual interdependence among the world's religions. He sees that an "actual impact of traditions on each other is clearly discernable in history," noting "Hinduism has directly influenced the rise of Buddhism," "Jainism, in its teaching of *ahimsa*, or nonharming, has influenced both Buddhism and Hinduism," "Christianity would hardly be possible without Judaism, and Islam is inconceivable without these predecessors." He cites a number of other examples in which this spiritual interdependence is evident among other traditions.

Teasdale coined the terms interspirituality and intermysticism to designate the increasingly familiar phenomenon of cross-religious sharing of the spiritual treasures of each tradition. He predicted this would become the norm in the future. And since all the world's religions are founded in an experience of mystical spirituality, this is not only a return to the inner essence of religion, it is also what can prepare the way for "a planet-wide enlightened culture."

Interspirituality itself, or the spiritual interdependence among the religions, Teasdale says, exists because an essential interconnectedness exists in all of reality. Thus, what is really needed is a universal spirituality that is holistic, integrative, and unifying, one that recognizes that we all have a much greater heritage than simply our own tradition. After all, this unity, this oneness, is the heart of all traditions, and the foundation for building a better world.

In response to Teasdale's identification of the Interspiritual Age, Kurt Johnson co-authored the popular and exhaustive book, *The Coming Interspiritual Age*, and established the Interspiritual Network, a growing movement of organizations and individuals exploring and embracing the emerging interspiritual paradigm, defined in part by the points of agreement that make up the Interspiritual Declaration.

The beginning of the 21st century and the new millennium saw a marked increase of interfaith, and what appears to be just the beginning of interspiritual, activities. In 2000, Episcopal Power and Light broadened its focus, brought in other faith partners, and became Interfaith Power and Light, the first multi-faith organization, now with forty state affiliate groups, to respond to global warming by being faithful stewards of Creation and growing a clean energy economy.

Inspired by the 1999 Parliament of the World's Religions in Cape Town, South Africa, and incorporated in 2002 by founder Eboo Patel, Interfaith Youth Core seeks cooperation among different religious and secular communities by developing interfaith leaders on college campuses that will later drive the dialogue of interfaith cooperation through the three core components of respect for religious identity, mutually inspiring relationships, and common action for the common good.

Also in 2002, the Universal House of Justice, the international governing council of the Baha'i Faith, issued a statement addressed to "The World's Religious Leaders," opening with the observation that events of the twentieth century have "compelled the peoples of the world to begin seeing themselves as the members of a single human race, and the earth as that race's common homeland."

The statement recalls Baha'u'llah's words of more than a century ago: "The peoples of the world, of whatever race or religion, derive their inspiration from one heavenly Source." The implication of this principle of the oneness of humanity – and of religion – is not to question one's "faith in the fundamental verities of any of the world's great belief systems," but rather to let go of all "claims to exclusivity or finality," which are what lead to hatred and violence.

This principle, instead, encourages a deeper exploration of humanity's common spiritual heritage, which is an expression, the statement adds, of "the principle of religion's evolutionary nature." This statement is a challenge to the interfaith movement to seriously consider the implications of this oneness.

In other words, the interspiritual age will really come into full swing when humanity finally and fully recognizes its oneness, when we realize our union with all of creation, and when we put this consciousness into action, as many already have. This is what all the spiritual forces in operation today are leading us toward, even though there are opposing forces at work in the world as well. The convergence of relatively recent scientific discoveries and the latest divine Revelation means that there is not only an inherent harmony between the two but that there are spiritual forces guiding this grand synthesis.

A Bridge Across the Ages & Traditions

Recalling humanity's three stages of evolution from chapter three, we have seen how we have moved from an inherent consciousness of oneness during our earliest years, to a prolonged childhood and adolescent period characterized by a consciousness of duality, and are now, as we enter our stage of maturity, making our way back to our intended consciousness of oneness. But it seems reasonable to ask how we will manage to make such a shift from duality to oneness after so many centuries of having become complacent with a dualistic worldview.

It appears that we need a bridge across the consciousness divide, across the sea of duality that has become so wide over the centuries as to seem impossible to cross. This needs to be a bridge that would link our emerging intended consciousness of oneness with our original inherent consciousness of oneness.

If we understand where we are today, and how we got here, currently striving to bring about world unity, we may recognize that there already exists three strong girders in this bridge over the sea of duality that can once and for all get humanity across this great divide to the other side.

The first girder of this bridge is the long chain of Indigenous peoples, who in earliest times lived with an inherent consciousness of oneness. Almost miraculously, their descendants, having struggled mightily for many millennia, across humanity's entire dualistic period, and under the most severe oppression, have maintained this consciousness of oneness, and are today passing this on to the world.

The survival and resurgence of this indigenous wisdom of oneness, harmony, and balance represents a crucial unbroken link in the great chain of being that has carried a holistic perspective on from earliest times to our time. This was nowhere more evident than at the 2015 Parliament of the World's Religions. Indigenous leaders from all corners of the globe shared their message of oneness in so many moving, powerful, and meaningful ways throughout this special gathering of people of faith from around the world, reminding everyone where we all came from, and what is needed to ensure our collective survival.

The world's religions hold a key role for prophesies of a promised time, as in the Gospel of St. Luke: "And they shall come from the east, and from the west, and from the north, and from the south, and shall sit down in the Kingdom of God."

The same is true of the Indigenous spiritual traditions, where a belief in the continuity and progressive nature of spiritual teachings is also key. From the Americas to the Pacific Islands and beyond, Indigenous teachings say we are now living in a time of fulfillment. Indigenous voices are speaking out, warning the world of the dangers we face and how we can avert disaster by living in harmony with one another.

Their message is clear and direct: we are in a time of purification that includes chaos and destruction; this is a time for the human race to realize its essential unity; in order to heal the damage done to Mother Earth, we must also realize that all living things are endowed with spirit; and, this is the time of the return of one or more of the Great Teachers who will guide us into the future.

In one of these Native traditions, Lakota leaders Black Elk and Crazy Horse in the late 1800s had powerful visions of the future. Black Elk thought his vision meant that a great Prophet from the East would bring a message to his people. And Crazy Horse saw dancing along with his people under the Sacred Tree representatives of all races who were working together to make the world whole again.

The second girder of this bridge across the sea of duality is the one built by the founders of the world's great religions. In each age, they have brought a single but progressively unfolding message focusing on the needs of the time in which it was revealed. The earliest Prophets focused on oneness within the family, the tribe, and the village, while later Prophets focused on oneness and unity within the city, the state, and the nation.

As we have seen, the Baha'i revelation, coming from the East, is focused on the consciousness of the oneness of humanity, the greatest need of our time, with supporting universal spiritual principles that will help usher in this age of world unity.

The reverberations resulting from the release of spiritual energies in each age have spread throughout the regions and the world, impacting areas and peoples well beyond their point of origin. This is a vital piece in the effectiveness and ultimate success of each revelation achieving its intended purpose of oneness and unity within its intended realm.

The third girder of this bridge is the interfaith, interspiritual, and social justice movements of the late 20th and early 21st centuries that have picked up and maintained the Perennial Philosophy, or the Great Chain of Being, and especially the Eastern philosophies of harmony and balance, that have also spanned the consciousness divide. Carrying these timeless and universal principles across this great divide has created another girder that cannot be denied in its essential contribution to re-establishing a consciousness of oneness.

Coming back to the principles underlying this book, the unfolding of human consciousness is a potentiality leading us to new capacities and new collective responsibilities. While life is caught up in the endless flow of opposites leading us to greater and greater levels of transformation, we must never lose sight of the love that is the underlying force of evolution, nor the justice that maintains the inherent balance of life.

This is all a grand evolutionary process under the guidance of the Creator that has brought us all to the recognition of oneness and the threshold of unity, global harmony, and peace. These core principles and spiritual forces shaping our time constitute a single, all-embracing vision of humanity's future that only we can ensure will become a reality in the world for our descendants.

We live in the day of fulfillment. This is the time when the way is being made ready for a new world, for the coming together of all the diverse peoples into one family, as in the sacred texts of old: "one fold, and one shepherd," (John 10:16); or, "the promised Day" (Qur'an 85:2).

This new creation is today everywhere evident, unfolding with a force subtle yet certain, just as a seedling in time becomes a fruit-bearing tree, or a child reaches adulthood. We are at a threshold never before crossed. Our collective coming-of-age as a single people is at hand.

As Oren Lyons noted, "We are the generation with the responsibility and option to choose the path with a future for our children. We must join hands with the rest of creation, and speak of common sense, responsibility, brotherhood, and peace."

The most important work today, the action most needed to be taken by each of us, is work across boundaries, across differences. Any step that can be taken in our regular, everyday interactions toward anyone different in any way than us is to remove barriers that have been put up between us by others. Joining hands across differences is the sacred activism of our time.

Anything that gets in the way of natural, compassionate, unconditional loving relationships and interactions is artificial. All the superficial, illusory boundaries, borders, and differences between us need to be consciously broken down, dismantled, and crossed so we can experience no separation between any of us, as human beings.

This is the one form of social and sacred activism that will go the farthest in healing the great divide between the human family, in helping to move us toward and live according to a consciousness of oneness, and that will help bridge the gap between separation and wholeness.

As greater numbers embrace an orientation of global citizenship, and as this is reflected in various spheres of action, from interpersonal to social, cultural, and economic affairs, a consciousness of oneness will become as commonly accepted in the near future as nationalism was in the past.

Epilogue

The Global Movement Of Our Time: Building A Culture of Oneness

God holds out an invitation to us –
an invitation... to wholeness that leads to flourishing for all of us...
Our planet will not survive if we cling to the verities of the past.
We must recognize that we are part of one group, one family –
the human family.

-Desmond Tutu

We stand now where two roads diverge.
But unlike the roads in Robert Frost's familiar poem, they are not equally fair.
The road we have long been traveling is deceptively easy, a smooth
superhighway on which we progress with great speed,
but at its end lies disaster.
The other fork of the road — the one less traveled by —
offers our last, our only chance
to reach a destination that assures the preservation of the earth.

-Rachel Carson

We have been created to reflect the perfection of creation. Individual and collective action aimed toward the betterment of humanity is the dire need of our time. Barbara Marx Hubbard knows who these activist individuals will be; she has identified "a new breed of global citizens" that she calls "conscious evolutionaries." They are found "in every faith, every tradition, every race, every culture, and every economic background." What distinguishes them is the quality of feeling "the emergent potential within" themselves; they are driven with a passion "toward self-evolution and self-expression for the sake of... the world."

To move from a consciousness of duality, where many cultures exist in conflict, to a consciousness of oneness, where many cultures exist in harmony, may not be as earth-shattering, challenging, or dramatic as it sounds. All it really requires is a shift of awareness toward a new and deeper understanding of our core nature of nonduality, where we recognize that reality is one, and that truth is indivisible. To see nonduality as the essence of all of existence enables us to adopt a *consciousness* of oneness, which is what will lead to a *culture* of oneness.

This is where we started as human beings. After many millennia of living in difficulty, dissension, and discord, humanity is now rediscovering a deep-seated desire to live in this world as one. A culture of oneness means living in unity within our multiplicity, honoring our diversity within our common heritage as human beings, and safeguarding our differences while recognizing we are more alike than unalike.

The crisis facing humanity is, ultimately, spiritual. Our greatest danger is complacency, remaining entrenched in a part-focused worldview. What is required is a change of consciousness, a spiritual transformation freeing ourselves from attachment to inherited assumptions and habits that no longer fit the needs of the day.

Our task in this emerging global age is re-conceptualizing everything we think we know anything about: the way we see the world, the way we understand reality, the way we understand human identity, the way we relate to one another and the earth we share, the way we approach science and religion, the way we understand the nature of conflict, the way we envision the journey of life, and, perhaps most of all, the way we see the very nature and purpose of divinity.

These shifts have already begun to happen, and on a global scale in both secular and sacred settings. Our progress over the past century has been in fits and starts, yet many of the above timeless spiritual principles can be seen working through the social, economic and political forces surrounding us.

The spiritual principles of our time, first seen in the 19th-century Revelation of Baha'u'llah, are already becoming almost second nature as we slowly but surely take on the identity of citizens of the world. Planetary consciousness, according to Ervin Laszlo, is "knowing, as well as feeling, the vital interdependence and essential oneness of humankind. It is the conscious adoption of the ethic and the ethos that this entails." The greatest need in our time is broadening our own personal identity to see ourselves as planetary citizens.

Martin Luther King, Jr. called for this wider identity over a half century ago, as well: "Every nation must now develop an overriding loyalty to mankind as a whole in order to preserve the best in their individual societies. This call for a worldwide fellowship that lifts neighborly concern beyond one's tribe, race, class, and nation is in reality a call for an all-embracing and unconditional love for all mankind."

Our challenge is to disregard the fleeting notions of the day, and instead recognize their sharp contrast to the overriding spiritual forces of our time. These are what are compelling us toward putting into action the principles needed for lasting collective security. This is what will lead to the realization of oneness, which would incorporate global justice, equity, unity, and finally world peace.

There are many already building out this vision. James O'Dea says each of us can help build a global culture of peace by becoming 21st century peace ambassadors. He takes a holistic approach, linking peace-building initiatives everywhere to a more comprehensive peace movement rooted in understanding the problem of violence.

Similarly, Barbara Marx Hubbard, taking a holistic approach focusing on each of us participating in humanity's birthing process "to the age of conscious evolution," might be seen as a role model for so many others. Her Foundation for Conscious Evolution includes a container for connecting and empowering global movements for positive change by forming evolutionary communities and evolutionary shift circles that focus on creating synergy with the One.

Communities of Action

So many initiatives and activities, too numerous to mention all of them, are beginning to transform this earth into a different world. A consciousness of oneness and the concept of world citizenship both embody the principle of service to humanity. As consciousness expands, so does the desire and potential for action. Higher levels of consciousness create wider and wider circles of affinity and attraction, begetting more champions of justice who help to create a just and inclusive social order.

In addition to the previously mentioned interfaith organizations, a few of the other groups and movements working to build a culture of oneness through a variety of approaches, listed in order of their origin, are:

- **Institute for Noetic Sciences:** an emerging movement of globally conscious citizens helping to birth a new worldview recognizing our basic interconnectedness and interdependence (1973), http://www.noetic.org.
- **New Seminary:** the oldest seminary of its kind in the world, ordaining interfaith ministers focusing on spiritual activism (1979), http://www.new-seminary.com.
- **Four Worlds International Institute:** utilizing Indigenous wisdom of the Fourth Way to unify the human family (1982), http://www.fwii.net.
- **Club of Budapest:** building a planetary consciousness through the vital interdependence and essential oneness of humankind, and by adopting the ethics and ethos this entails (1996), http://www.clubofbudapest.org.
- **Chaplaincy Institute** of California (1999), http://chaplaincyinstitute.org, and **Chaplaincy Institute of Maine (ChIME,** 2002), http://chimeofmaine.org, educating, training, and ordaining interfaith chaplains and leaders.
- **Oneness:** eliminating racism and promoting unity through music, the arts and education (1999), http://www.oneness.org.
- **New Stories:** serving as a collaboratory of people and projects nurturing the emergence of new stories for who we are as humanity,

and what we can become together (2000), http://www.newstories.
org.

- **One Spirit Interfaith Seminary:** a leader in interspiritual education, training, and ordination (2002), http://onespiritinterfaith.org.
- **Humanity's Team:** a movement intending to awaken the world to Oneness in a generation, so children will grow up in a very different world (2003), http://www.humanitysteam.org.
- **ONE:** taking action to end extreme poverty and preventable disease, particularly in Africa (2005), https://www.one.org/us.
- **Evolutionary Leaders:** engaging our collective field of potential in a movement to ignite an evolutionary leap to the next level of human consciousness (2008), http://www.evolutionaryleaders.net.
- **National Peace Academy:** advancing the transformation to a culture of peace in the US and the world by elevating in the public consciousness the meaning and value of peacebuilding (2009), http://nationalpeaceacademy.us.
- **Charter for Compassion:** urging a global perspective in honoring the sanctity of every single human being based on the principles of universal justice, equity, and respect (2009), http://www.charterforcompassion.org.
- **The Shift Network:** empowering a global movement of people creating an evolutionary shift of consciousness leading to a more enlightened society (2010), http://theshiftnetwork.com.
- **Uplift:** engaging a global community committed to co-creating oneness in action in the world (2012), http://upliftconnect.com.
- **The Interspiritual Network:** organizations and individuals exploring and embracing the emerging Interspiritual paradigm for authentic understanding, collaboration and practice (2013), http://interspirituality.com.

Attending the 2015 Parliament of the World's Religions – *Reclaiming the Heart of Our Humanity, Working Together for a World of Compassion, Peace, Justice, and Sustainability* – was an experience like none other in my life. With the Parliament, and the world, having evolved significantly over the past 122 years, there was no group that was overlooked or excluded at this Parliament. 10,000 people from 50 faith communities and persuasions spent five days together finding more common ground than might have otherwise taken a lifetime to accomplish.

Everyone was welcomed into the sprawling convention center by indigenous tribal members who lit a Sacred Fire just outside the main entrance at a sunrise ceremony on the first day; they kept it going for five days. Indigenous leaders from all continents also brought a strong, much-needed presence to many plenary sessions and other programs with heartfelt messages of concern for our Mother Earth and a need for harmony and balance to sustain our relationship with her.

Every day, for those thousands from any background that wanted it, scores of members of the international Sikh community prepared and served langar, a free but surely sacred lunch, as row upon row of shoeless participants with white head coverings sat on the floor in reverence and appreciation for the meal they received with such respect. Also going on throughout the Parliament were the Mandala Sand Paintings by Tibetan Buddhist monks, one for world peace and one for the long life and honor of His Holiness the Dalai Lama, not attending because of health issues.

I felt honored to be able to present a paper there, a variation of a section of chapter three from this book, on the evolution of justice. It felt appropriate to begin with the Golden Rule as the universal expression of a principle of justice that is needed as much today on the global level as it always has been on the interpersonal level, and to conclude with the thought that justice is the unifying force expressed in every dimension of reality though this can only be seen with the eye of oneness.

There were so many moments of breakthrough, connection, unity, and wonderment in so many places it is hard to imagine that this spirit of oneness will not carry on from this gathering. A few of the gems of truth that were spoken include:

- "I don't care what part of our Mother you come from, we are one" (Dr. Rangimarie Turuki Rose Pere, Maori Elder);
- "Working on climate change without paradigm change would be a

grave mistake" (Steven Newcomb, Shawnee, Lenape author);

- "Whatever faith you grow up in, it's all one God... The children and young people give me the most hope, and also the indomitable human spirit" (Jane Goodall, United Nations Messenger of Peace);
- "Diversity is the most important element of nature... Work hard for the children, work hard for the future" (Oren Lyons, Seneca Elder);
- "We've got to reclaim our soul... We all have the same heart; I believe it will be the young people to make the link between head and heart" (Mary Maguire, Nobel Peace Laureate).

The world is moving closer to putting into practice the cornerstone principle of the oneness of humanity. The means to achieve these goals are at our fingertips. Numerous other initiatives and activities are also underway. The United Nations itself has long been engaged in activities designed to move the world toward unity.

Recent efforts, such as the United Nations Millennium Development Goals to eradicate extreme poverty and hunger, achieve universal primary education, promote gender equality and empower women, reduce child mortality, improve maternal health, combat HIV/AIDS, Malaria, and other diseases, ensure environmental sustainability, and global partnerships for development are all necessary for ensuring a life of dignity for all and the well-being of the planet.

COP21, the 2015 United Nations Climate Change Conference held in Paris just a few months after the Parliament of the World's Religions, brought together the world's political leaders (the European Union and 195 nations), NGOs (Non-Governmental Organizations), indigenous community leaders, and faith communities to agree by consensus to a global pact reducing greenhouse gas. The role each one of these groups played in making possible such an accord to protect the future of the planet itself *and* quicken the process of all peoples coming to a consciousness of oneness cannot be denied.

The literally millions of NGOs worldwide are regularly carrying out acts of compassion and altruistic service that promote the general welfare of humanity. These can each be seen as the ultimate expression of a consciousness of oneness.

Every faith community has its initiatives and projects designed to bring about the betterment of the world. The overwhelming number of these efforts in every part of the world contribute to a culture of service, helping overcome a culture of violence and prejudice, in turn helping to establish a culture of economic equity, racial unity, and, ultimately, oneness.

The vast and ever-expanding sea of women and men from virtually every faith community and every culture, ethnicity, and nation who serve the various agencies of the United Nations, their affiliated Non-Governmental Organizations, and the secular or independent groups and projects that put the good of the whole first, all of these represent an ever-expanding planetary "civil service" who express the highest commitment to global cooperation ever seen. In Desmond Tutu's wise words, "Each year we inch toward a more perfect way of living as a global community."

These efforts, and many more, are having a cumulative effect on humanity's consciousness; its transformation is well underway. All that remains for the fulfillment of the vision of oneness to be realized is continued action and service toward its end, toward "better mutual understanding, as well as to socially-beneficial, peace-fostering and Earth-friendly ways of life."

Appendix I

A Timeline of Humanity's Conscious Evolution

While forces of integration and separation have been at play throughout history, this timeline intends to briefly summarize the continuous nature of the force of integration in guiding humanity's advancement toward a consciousness of oneness. **Bold** represents major leaps in human consciousness; c. represents an approximate time.

Prehistory	**The Indigenous & Ancient Spiritual Traditions Era (origin of the Indigenous branch of religion),** all continents, each with their own spiritual Teachers (including shamanism and ancient mystery schools). Tribal histories preserved names and teachings focusing on harmony, balance, and oneness.
c.1800 BCE	**The Hebrew/Judaic Era (origin of the Abrahamic branch of religion),** in Ur, with the Revelation of Abraham, who established a covenant with, and a belief in the oneness of, God, and later (c.1300 BCE) at Mount Sinai, with the Revelation of Moses (the *Torah*), which focused on justice, moral conduct, service, and the oneness of the family and tribe.

c.1500 BCE   **The Vedic/Hindu Era (origin of the Dharmic branch of religion)**, in India, with many spiritual Teachers. Vedic tribal histories compiled beliefs, practices, and deities into hymns (the *Rig Veda*), representing cosmic order. By c.700 BCE, the *Upanishads* (or Vedanta, meaning end of the *Vedas*) formed classical Hinduism. The *Bhagavad Gita* (c.400 BCE), with Krishna as the spiritual Teacher emphasizing oneness with Brahman (Ultimate Reality), has become one of the world's most influential sacred works.

c.1100 BCE   The *I Ching* (Book of Changes), focusing on following the Tao (Way), influenced all of Chinese spirituality.

c.1000 BCE   **The Zoroastrian Era**, in Persia, with the Revelation of Zoroaster (the *Avesta*), brought a new level of spiritual discipline, ethical consciousness, and justice, the basis of a great civilization.

c.580 BCE   The Taoist tradition, in China, with the teachings of Lao Tzu (the *Tao Te Ching*), came during a time of social and political turmoil, emphasizing wholeness (with yin-yang being not just polarities but a representation of the nondual whole); this influenced the entire social and cultural life of China, including Zen Buddhism.

c.560 BCE   **The Buddhist Era**, in India, with the teachings of Siddhartha Gautama (the *Dhammapada*), emphasized gaining release from suffering (*dukha*), living by the Middle Way (moderation), and treading the noble eightfold path. The Buddha's teachings have advanced humanity's understanding of liberating practices, mindfulness, compassion, ethical principles, and service to others.

c.557 BCE   The Jain tradition, in India, with the teachings of Mahavira (the *Kalpasutra*) included the Many-sidedness of Truth (similar to the Middle Way), Non-violence (*ahimsa*), and the divine nature of the soul. Jain teachings have greatly influenced Indian spiritual life.

c.500 BCE   The Confucian tradition, in China, with the teachings of Confucius (the *Analects*) who renewed the wisdom of the Ancients, emphasizing morality on all levels, justice, goodness, and harmony, and influencing greatly Chinese culture and religion.

c.570-c.322 BCE   The Greek Philosophers, from Pythagorus to Heraclitus, Socrates, Plato and Aristotle, were masters of uniting metaphysics, mystical insight, psychological acuity and the spirit of science to produce an integral understanding that has taken two millennia to match.

1 CE   **The Christian Era**, in Galilee, with the teachings of Jesus (sayings and parables preserved as part of the *Gospels*). Exemplified God's love for all, and taught that the kingdom of God is always present within all. By its 3rd century, Christianity became the dominant religion of the Roman Empire, and within two millennia the most populous in the world. Jesus' teachings were aimed at creating unity at the then prevailing social level of the city-state.

426 CE   St. Augustine taught the inherent unity of body and soul, leading many clergy under his authority to free their slaves "as an act of piety." He wrote in *The City of God* that slavery was contrary to God's divine plan.

c.500-c.1580 CE   The Christian Mystics, including Hildegard of Bingen, St. Francis of Assisi, Meister Eckhart, St. Teresa of Avila, and St. John of the Cross, all sought oneness with the Creator and the creation.

622 CE   **The Islamic Era**, in Mecca, with the Revelation of Muhammad (the *Qur'an*), focusing on submission to the will of God, conveyed a universality in accepting the previous Abrahamic prophets (Moses, Jesus, and others); particularly inspiring to the Sufis, who sought to the inner meaning of the Qur'an. Muhammad's revelation released a spiritual impulse that unified scattered tribal and desert people into a thriving Islamic national empire.

c.712   The Shinto tradition, in Japan, a blend of Hindu, Buddhist, Confucian, Taoist, Abrahamic, and secular beliefs, was guided by a worldview of awe and gratitude for a sacred cosmos.

c.750-c.1500   The Sufi Mystics, including Rabia, Al-Hallaj, Al-Ghazali, Avicenna, Averroes, Al-Arabi, Rumi, Hafiz, and Kabir, were all integral visionaries who sought union and oneness with the One in all things. Their ecstatic verses still contribute to the conscious evolution of increasing numbers into the 20th and 21st centuries.

c.800   Shankara, Vedanta sage, expounded the nondual ideal.

c.1380   The Renaissance, in Europe, was a revival of classical literature, law, aesthetics, and ethics encouraging a humanistic integral approach, as with Botticelli, Michelangelo, and Leonardo de Vinci, that brought science, art, and spirituality together to form a new consciousness of beauty, goodness, and human potential.

c.1490   The Sikh tradition, in India, with the teachings of Guru Nanak, emerging out of Hindu and Muslim influences. Sikh traditions emphasize contributing to the welfare of the community (extending to all of humanity), as with the *langar* (free meals to all).

c.1715   The Enlightenment, in Europe, rejected oppression of all kinds and shone a light on distinctions between reason and faith as never before. Advances in science and the apparent stagnation of religion pushed faith to the background and expanded the use of the scientific method, inadvertently opening the door to a new unifying vision that would reconcile the two knowledge systems.

1774   The Royal Humane Society, in England, inaugurated a trend toward humanitarianism, compassion, and justice, followed by the Red Cross movement and the Salvation Army in the mid 1800s.

Early 1800s   The German idealists (Schelling, Hegel, and Fichte) merged their musings with new scientific evidence of the earth as millions of years older than thought, giving rise to a new way thinking about the idea of inevitable progress, the divine spirit in all things, and transcendence, inspiring, in part, Transcendentalism in America.

1844	**The Babi Era** in Iran, with the Revelation of the Bab ("the Gate"), the herald of the Baha'i Faith. In a turbulent time when his country was undergoing widespread moral breakdown, the Bab brought a message of spiritual renewal, including improving the position of women and the poor, and that his mission was to prepare the way for the coming of a Manifestation of God who would usher in the age of peace and justice promised by the world's religions. He was executed in 1850 for his teachings.
1848	The Women's Rights Movement, in the U.S., began.
1852	**The Baha'i Era**, in Iran, with the Revelation of Baha'u'llah (the "Glory of God"), the Promised One foretold by the Bab. During 40 years of exile and persecution, thousands of verses, letters, tablets, and books flowed from His pen, releasing spiritual energies not yet seen or felt in this world. This extensive revelation ranged from a deeper understanding of living the spiritual life to a framework for developing a global civilization founded upon the spiritual principle of the oneness of humanity, supported by a series of interdependent principles (including the equality of women and men, the elimination of extremes of poverty and wealth, and the harmony of science and religion) necessary to bring about social justice, unity, and peace on the grandest scale. A century and three-

quarters later, the Baha'i Faith is established in every country and territory of the world.

1859 Charles Darwin's *The Origin of Species* made the discussion of biological evolution public, opening the door to all other forms of evolution (from social to cultural to religious), while also opening the door to understanding the harmony of science and religion, by making it scientifically accepted that all life comes from the same source, and is part of the great Tree of Life.

1860s Altruism and the principle of the oneness of humanity are moved closer to their potential with the Emancipation Proclamation, the 13th, 14th, and 15th Amendments, and the first Civil Rights Acts.

1893 The first Parliament of the World's Religions, in Chicago, offered a universal platform for many religious traditions new to America, with a challenge to 'return to the primitive unity of the world.' Swami Vivekananda addressed the Parliament saying, 'Science is nothing but the finding of unity... through multiplicity and duality the ultimate unity is reached.'

1911 John Muir, naturalist, noted that all things are hitched to everything else in the universe.

1911-13 Abdu'l-Baha, son of Baha'u'llah and authorized interpreter of the Baha'i writings, traveled throughout Europe and from coast to coast in North America speaking in churches, universities, and public halls on the ideals of women's rights, racial equality, social justice, unity, and peace, meeting people of all ranks and stations.

1912   Wilhelm Wundt, founder of experimental psychology, in *Elements of Folk Psychology*, presented a detailed outline of how the psychological and cultural development of humanity has been evolving toward a consciousness of 'mankind as a unity.'

1912   Helen Keller wrote, "When indeed shall we learn that we are all related one to the other, that we are all members of one body?"

1912   Booker T. Washington, educator, said, "We must learn to think not in terms of race or color or language or religion or of political boundaries, but in terms of humanity."

1920   The League of Nations, the first intergovernmental organization established to maintain world peace, was founded in Geneva.

1928   C.G. Jung, founder of analytic psychology, further shifted the focus to the collective, emphasizing the universal forces in the mind, or archetypes, that expand consciousness toward latent creativity, a holistic perspective, and spiritual realms. In "The Spiritual Problem of Modern Man," he noted 'We are only at the threshold of a new spiritual epoch.'

1930   Black Elk saw in his life-changing vision that all things "must live together like one being," and that the "many hoops" of many peoples "made one circle."

1936	The World Congress of Faiths convened in London.
1940	Pierre Teilhard de Chardin, Jesuit priest, said evolution and consciousness are ever advancing, and will eventually affirm the interconnectedness of all elements in the cosmos.
1944	Max Planck, father of quantum theory and Nobel Prize winner, said that behind the existence of all matter is an intelligent Mind.
1945	Aldous Huxley, in *The Perennial Philosophy*, identified the common ideas, principles, and values shared by all humanity across time.
1948	The Universal Declaration of Human Rights is adopted by the United Nations General Assembly.
1954-68	Continuing what began a century earlier, the U.S. Civil Rights Movement and five more Civil Rights Acts banned discrimination based on race, color, religion, sex, or national origin.
1960	The Temple of Understanding was founded by Juliet Hollister in New York City to draw people of all faiths together in unity.
1966	The Vatican II declaration, *Nostra Aetate*, created the framework for greater interreligious dialogue.
1966	Erik Erikson, developmental psychologist, said humanity's task now is to move beyond an identity built upon exclusivity to create instead a new, wider, all-inclusive, all-human identity.

1969	The first moonwalk captured humanity's attention with photos of its boundaryless homeland.
1973	The Institute for Noetic Sciences was founded by astronaut Edgar Mitchell to help birth a new consciousness of interconnectedness.
1979	The New Seminary was founded as the first interfaith seminary.
1982	David Bohm, quantum theorist, said, "deep down the consciousness of mankind is one."
1985	The Universal House of Justice, the international governing council of the Baha'i Faith, issued *The Promise of World Peace* to the peoples of the world.
1993	The 2nd Parliament of the World's Religions held in Chicago, drew an even greater diversity of spiritual traditions, and a Declaration on *A Global Ethic* is released.
1993	United Religions Initiative founded for interfaith bridge-building.
1996	The Club of Budapest, founded by Ervin Laszlo, to help build the emerging planetary consciousness of the oneness of humankind.
1998	Barbara Marx Hubbard, futurist, said we are in the midst of a great shift in consciousness, toward the planetary birth.

1999	Brother Wayne Teasdale, in *The Mystic Heart*, said we are at the dawn of the Interspiritual Age.
2000	UN Secretary-General Kofi Annan invited a Statement for the United Nations Millennium Summit, signed by over one thousand NGOs, that stated, "...We are one human family, in all our diversity, living on one common homeland..."
2003	PBS produced *Race: The Power of an Illusion*, tracing a concept that kept us apart but is now bringing us together as a human family.
2010	The Shift Network founded by Stephen Dinan to empower a global movement creating a shift of consciousness.
2011	At a press conference after the Japan earthquake, President Obama noted, "For all our differences in culture or language or religion, ultimately, humanity is one."
2015	The sixth Parliament of the World's Religions, in Salt Lake City, brought 10,000 people of every background together in harmony, and issued Declarations on *Climate Change*; *Hate Speech, War & Violence*; *Income Inequality*; *Human Rights & the Dignity of Women*; and, *Indigenous Peoples*.

Appendix II

A Meditation
For Living in Oneness

Right mindfulness, a foundation of Buddhist practice, as the seventh part of the Eightfold Path, can be used to transform our consciousness. It consists of being fully present, not judging, and witnessing everything as it is. A sustained awareness of the four foundations of mindfulness – a) the body, b) feelings and emotions, c) mental states (sleepy, restless, etc.), and, d) the way all things inter-exist (natural law) – can help change the mind's habits, ultimately assisting us to tap into an eternal wellspring of wisdom. A constant vigilance of these body/mind interactions can enable us to choose to re-pattern our thinking and create new ways of seeing the world, speaking about it, and acting in it. If we think, speak, or act with a peaceful mind, we become that peace. If we think, speak, and act with a consciousness of oneness, if we establish the habit of seeing all things with the eye of oneness, we will create a pattern that enables us to live in this oneness.

The regular and sustained practice of meditation can change what we think, experience, and envision; how long it takes to achieve this transformation of consciousness depends upon our commitment to the process. Here is a two-part meditation designed to lead us to a sustained consciousness of oneness. Set a timer for each part, as indicated.

Part 1

Part 1 is designed to bring about the inner peace that can be experienced when we are still, with a quiet mind; it will take less than two minutes.

Find a quiet place where you can relax, let go completely, and be with your inner thoughts. When you are ready, close your eyes, and just focus on your breathing – the in-breath, and the out-breath; the in-breath and the out-breath. Allow each breath that you take to bring you further and deeper into relaxation. Allow each part of yourself to feel this relaxation, your shoulders, arms, torso, legs, feet, and every muscle in your body. Now, allow your thoughts to flow freely through your relaxed mind, as leaves being blown along a woodland trail, for two minutes. Then, open your eyes, and reflect on the nature of those thoughts. Were they agreeable or disagreeable? Were they happy or sad thoughts? Reflect on what you'd like to do with this new awareness of your thoughts.

Part 2

Part 2 is designed to help you feel more connected to the greater whole, give you a deeper sense of unity with all things, and promote a feeling of peace and love for – and from – all things; it will take about 15 minutes, and can be repeated daily.

After you've had enough time to reflect on this new awareness of your thoughts, return to that quiet place where you can relax, and let go completely. When you are ready, close your eyes, and just breathe naturally, not trying to control the breath, but aware of the in-breath and the out-breath. Allow each breath to bring you deeper into relaxation. Feel this relaxation in your shoulders, back, arms, legs, and every muscle, fiber, and cell in your body.

Now, imagine that you are starting out on a journey from separation to union. Your soul, that eternal part of yourself, is traveling with your body, the temporal part of yourself. The body, with its limited mind, experiences the dualities of this world, goes back and forth between them, and is self-centered. The soul, with the power the Spirit, knows the oneness of all things. In this state, the body and the soul are separate from each other. Yet, the goal of their journey together is to experience the oneness that pervades all of creation.

As you feel the relaxation of your entire body, become aware of your heart, and feel the love always emanating from your heart. This love always in your heart is the love that connects you – as a living, breathing co-creator – to all other created beings, eliminates all forms of prejudice, and unifies the entire creation. With this universal, altruistic, unconditional love, there is no room in your heart for anything else. Imagine this deep, eternal love spreading out from your heart to all things around you, and to all things far from you. Take a minute to just really feel in your depths the power of this love spreading from you throughout the neighborhood, the country, the world, and the universe to all forms of life, the animals, the plants, the stars. Then, let this love flow back into your heart, and feel the true joy, true ecstasy, that this brings you.

As this new feeling of unconditional love brings you out of doubt and into certitude, your inner eyes are opened to a new reality where you recognize providence in all things and the inner significance of all things. Creation is seen in its perfect form, as a unified whole, and as sanctified in all its parts. Justice is understood as an eternal law, grace as ever present, and divine wisdom as an eternal wellspring, continuous and never-ending.

Passing beyond the last plane of limitation, you come to know there is no separation between you and the whole, and no distinction to be made between any of its parts. The entire creation is one, reality is one, and our conscious evolution is purposeful, leading us to a long-promised stage of human maturity where all will be as it was meant to be, all things flowing together in their intended harmony. Reflect deeply for a couple of minutes on what this feels like to you.

This is your new challenge, staying with this subjective understanding of the deep, organic, all-pervading unity of all created things. The oneness of creation – and its sanctity – is the consciousness that has been longed for and is now real.

To live with – and within – this consciousness of oneness is to remember at all times, especially when most difficult, that we are all interconnected, all one. This sense of divine unity, of inherent oneness, may not have come easily, but is the result of opposing forces finally having been merged into a greater whole. Remember that it has most likely taken a true transformation to achieve this awareness. Take a few minutes now to reflect as deeply as possible on what it will take for you to sustain this awareness of oneness throughout all the changing circumstances of your life. This is the time to really examine what and how much this consciousness of oneness means to you, what challenges it might present to you, and how you can sustain it.

Beyond this knowledge of oneness is putting it into action in every way and every aspect of your life. Living in and with a consciousness of oneness includes letting the world of the flesh give way to the world of the spirit, as a heart filled with divine love sees only oneness. Differences are accepted for what they are, and the spiritual qualities of humility, respect for all creatures, and a more intense desire to experience unity in diversity rise to the surface. Take another few minutes to reflect on what it would be like for you to put this consciousness of oneness into action in your everyday life, and especially reflect on how you can see yourself maintaining this over the remaining years of your life.

As your soul progresses in its development, which is on-going, your body, mind, and soul will more often function as one, as a unity more decisively led by your soul. This progress brings greater contentment and inner peace, more easily resolved tensions, and a greater capacity for service to humanity.

Now, finally, take as much time as you need to reflect more deeply on how you might be able to more fully manifest your altruistic love in the world, and how you will be able to express your much needed awareness of the consciousness of oneness to others in your regular interactions.

When your reflections come to a close, open your eyes, come back to the present, and write down all the new thoughts you've had during this meditation to keep with you and to refer to as often as needed.

Acknowledgments

Story may well be the most important thing in our lives, after relationships. All good, sacred stories are about relationships of one kind or another, and the story behind *The Story of Our Time* is no different.

I first want to thank my earliest mentors, Pete Seeger and Joseph Campbell, who helped clear my path to recognizing the interconnectedness of all things, with their words *and* deeds. I am also indebted to the pioneering integrative work of Guy Murchie, Nat Rutstein, Hooper Dunbar, Suheil Bushrui, and John Hatcher, who helped make the pieces of the larger whole fit together more perfectly.

Among those who have also inspired this work in various ways at different points are Ervin Laszlo, Barbara Marx Hubbard, Duane Elgin, Peter Adriance, Sovaida Maani Ewing, Julio Savi, and Barney Leith.

I am very grateful to Martha Schweitz, Jane Harper, and Kate Weisman for bringing their discerning eye to the manuscript, and for offering vital insights. I'd also like to thank Pamela Wilson, Dana Sawyer, Betty and Noel Stookey, Jacob Watson, Glenn and Linda Nerbak, Dan Trollinger, Kathleen Scacciaferro, Phyllis Ring, Kit Bigelow, and David Henderson for their supportive thoughts and feedback, as well.

For her contribution to the book cover design, I am deeply grateful to Tamera Cooke, whose beautiful mandala of nine flames represent the unity of the world's religions, at the center of which is seen the One Source from which they all originate.

I could not have found a better fit for editor of this work than Kate Sheehan Roach. From the moment we fortuitously met at the Parliament of the World's Religions, she has been an advocate for my work, an astute editor for my blog at Patheos.com, and now the purveyor of the perfect perspective, insights, and support to bring this book to its intended audience. I am deeply grateful for all of her contributions to the book.

For taking time out of their busy schedules to add their endorsements to the book, those who I haven't already mentioned, I extend my deepest gratitude to Michael Bernard Beckwith, Kurt Johnson, Mirabai Starr, Larry Dossey, Llewellyn Vaughn-Lee, Philip Goldberg, Rabbi Rami Shapiro, Rev. Cynthia Bourgeault, Lewis Mehl-Madrona, Rhett Diessner, and Kevin Locke.

I am also extremely grateful to have found Rev. Patricia Cagganello, Maryanne Corey, and Sacred Stories Publishing. They have been an absolute pleasure and delight to partner with on this book, and I thank them for their wonderful work, and most especially their full commitment to this project and their sustained support in carrying it out.

Most of all, my deepest appreciation and lasting gratitude goes to Cynthia, for always being there, and for reading what I write with such understanding, detachment, honesty, and wisdom.

Endnotes

PROLOGUE

i   Ethan Siegal, "What Is The Most Astounding Fact About the Universe?" in *Forbes/Science*, April 8, 2016 http://www.forbes.com/sites/startswithabang/2016/04/08/what-is-the-most-astounding-fact-about-the-universe/#3d6f8121144b; see also Abdu'l-Baha, *Some Answered Questions* (Wilmette, IL: Baha'i Publishing Trust, 1987), 3.

ii   Pierre Teilhard de Chardin, *The Human Phenomenon*, translated by Sarah Appleton-Weber (Portland, OR: Sussex Academic Press, 2003).

ii   Abdu'l-Baha, *Foundations of World Unity* (Wilmette, IL: Baha'i Publishing Trust, 1979), 12. Abdu'l-Baha was the son and successor of Baha'u'llah ("Glory of God"), the latest in a long line of divine Educators – known as Manifestations of God, and the founder of the Baha'i Faith. The Baha'i era refers to when the Baha'i Faith came into being in 1844 in Persia, what is now Iran. Baha'is believe that throughout history God has sent to humanity spiritual teachers who have provided the basis for the advancement of civilization, and who have all come from the same Source, in essence bringing successive chapters in the religion of God. Baha'u'llah's extensive Revelation, numbering thousands of verses, letters, and books that flowed directly from His pen during the years 1852-1892, develops the theme of oneness and unity on all levels from the individual, to the family, community, and a peaceful and unified global civilization. At his passing in 1921, Abdu'l-Baha named his grandson, Shoghi Effendi, as the guardian and authorized interpreter of the teachings of Baha'u'llah. He established the framework for the election of the Universal House of Justice in 1963, which today guides the Baha'i international community, currently established in more than 100,000 localities in virtually every country and territory in the world, in contributing to the betterment of the world.

ii-iii   **Give us security**: Anne Wilson Schaef, *Native Wisdom for White*

Minds (New York: One World/Ballantine Books, 1995), July 23.

iii   Helen Keller, quoted in Dorothy Herrmann, *Helen Keller: A Life* (Chicago: University of Chicago Press, 1999), 344.

iii   **World order**: Universal House of Justice, *The Promise of World Peace* (Haifa: Baha'i World Centre, 1985), 10.

INTRODUCTION

v   Max Planck, the father of Quantum Theory and Nobel prize winner, from an address delivered in Florence, Italy, 1944, entitled "The Essence of Matter," quoted in Gregg Braden, *The Divine Matrix*. Carlsbad: Hay House, 2007, p.216, and also referenced on his website: http://www.greggbraden.com/resources/technical_references.

vi   **Beginning, muddle, and resolution**, what I have referred to as the sacred pattern of story, or the blueprint for psychospiritual development, is meant to guide and bring about psychological and spiritual transformation. This pattern is the spiritual equivalent of the genome, or the genetic program of the species, in this case a developmental program within us that is designed to enable us to stay on the developmental path we are meant to be on. Robert Atkinson, *The Gift of Stories: Practical and Spiritual Applications of Autobiography, Life Stories, and Personal Mythmaking* (Westport, CT: Bergin & Garvey, 1995).

vi   C.G. Jung, *Memories, Dreams, Reflections* (New York: Vintage Books, 1961), 332.

vi   See Sidney Liebes, Elisabet Sahtouris, and Brian Swimme, *A Walk Through Time: From Stardust to Us – The Evolution of Life on Earth* (Hoboken, NJ: John Wiley & Sons, 1998); also the website: http://globalcommunity.org/multimedia.shtml for the video, "An Extraordinary Moment."

vii   Thomas Berry, "The Cosmology of Religions and the Sacred Story of the Universe," in Joel Beversluis, ed., *Sourcebook of the World's Religions* (Novato, CA: New World Library, 2000), 244-9.

ix   **Evolutionary universe**: Thomas Berry, *ibid.*

ix   Brian Swimme, see: http://www.azquotes.com/author/43588-Brian_Swimme.

x   Ervin Laszlo, *Science and the Akashic Field: An Integral Theory of*

Everything (Rochester, VT: Inner Traditions International, 2004).

x   See Arthur O. Lovejoy, *The Great Chain of Being: The History of an Idea* (Cambridge: Harvard University Press, 1964); Aldous Huxley, *The Perennial Philosophy* (New York: Harper & Row, 1945); and, Ken Wilber, *Sex, Ecology, Spirituality: The Spirit of Evolution* (Boston: Shambhala, 1995), Ch. 1.

x   Pierre Tielhard de Chardin, *The Phenomenon of Man* (New York: Perennial, 1976), 300-304; and, *Toward the Future* (New York: Harvest/HBJ, 2002), 13, 114-117.

xiii   **7 principles**: for sources and references for each of these, see the beginning of each chapter.

xiv   **Ultimate Reality**: Suheil Bushrui and Mehrdad Massoudi, *The Spiritual Heritage of the Human Race* (Oxford: Oneworld Publications, 2010), 5-6.

xv   **Experience of unity**: Wayne Teasdale, *The Mystic Heart: Discovering a Universal Spirituality in the World's Religions* (Novato, CA: New World Library, 1999), 27-28; 212-216.

xvi   Wayne Teasdale, ibid., 4-7.

xvi   Baha'u'llah, *Gleanings From the Writings of Baha'u'llah* (Wilmette, IL: Baha'i Publishing Trust, 1990), 250.

xvi   Shoghi Effendi, quoted from the U.S. *Baha'i News*, No. 102, August 1936, p.3. http://www.bahai.org/library/authoritative-texts/the-universal-house-of-justice/messages/#d=19840612_001&f=f1-10

xvi   **Thousandfold increase**: Guy Murchie, *The Seven Mysteries of Life: An Exploration of Science and Philosophy* (New York: Houghton Mifflin, 1978), 569-586.

xvii   Swami Vivekananda, http://vivekananda.org/readings.asp.

xvii   **Birth of the interfaith movement**: *2015 Parliament of the World's Religions Salt Lake* Program (Chicago: Parliament of the World's Religions, 2015) 8.

xvii   John Henry Barrows: http://www.parliamentofreligions.org/parliament/chicago-1893

xviii   Chief Oren Lyons, quoted in Kim Lim, *1001 Pearls of Spiritual Wisdom* (New York: Skyhorse Publishing, 2014), 286.

1. OUR INHERENT URGE TO UNDERSTAND REALITY

1   Gregory Bateson, *Mind and Nature: A Necessary Unity* (New York: Bantam Books, 1988).

1   St. Teresa of Avila, *Let Nothing Disturb You*, edited by John Kirvan (Notre Dame, IN: Ave Maria Press, 2008).

1   Bede Griffiths, *A New Vision of Reality: Western Science, Eastern Mysticism and Christian Faith* (Springfield, IL: Templegate Publishers, 1990).

3   **Principle 1**: see Abdu'l-Baha, *Promulgation of Universal Peace* (Wilmette, IL: Baha'i Publishing Trust, 1982), 180; *Century of Light,* prepared under the supervision of The Universal House of Justice (Haifa: Baha'i World Centre, 2001), 39, 138; Baha'i International Community, *The Prosperity of Humankind* (Haifa: Baha'i World Center, 1995), 6, 10.

4   Rumi, *Love is a Stranger: Selected Lyric Poetry of Jalal al-Din Rumi* Translated by Kabir Helminski (Boston: Shambhala, 2000).

5   Walt Whitman, "Song of the Open Road," *Leaves of Grass* (New York: Dover, 2007).

5   Friedrich Nietzsche, *Twilight of the Idols,* trans. R. J. Hollingdale. (New York: Penguin Books, 1990), "Maxims and Arrows," #12).

5   Joni Mitchell, "Urge for Going," *Hits* Warner Bros. CD, 1996.

6   Elizabeth Gilbert, *Eat, Pray, Love: One Woman's Search for Everything Across Italy, India, and Indonesia* (New York: Penguin, 2007), 154.

6   Shankara, quoted in Aldous Huxley, *The Perennial Philosophy*, 7.

7   Evelyn Underhill, *Mysticism* (New York: Dutton, 1961), 445.

7   Joseph Campbell, *The Hero With a Thousand Faces* (New York: Meridian Books, 1949), 49-68; see also Robert Atkinson, *The Gift of Stories*.

7   Evelyn Underhill, ibid, 3, 176.

8   Baha'u'llah, *The Seven Valleys and the Four Valleys* (Wilmette, IL: Baha'i Publishing Trust, 1975), 5-7; Baha'u'llah, *Gems of Divine Mysteries* (Haifa: Baha'i World Center, 2002), 27-8.

8   Carl Jung, *Psychological Reflections* (Princeton: Princeton University Press, 1973), 22, 29-31; "The Structure of the Psyche," *Collected Works*, Vol. 8, par. 342.

9   **Mind is the intermediary**: Abdu'l-Baha, *Some Answered Questions* (Wilmette, IL: Baha'i Publishing Trust, 1987), 210-11.

9   **Free will**: Abdu'l-Baha, ibid, 248-50.

10   **Conditions for growth**: Deepak Chopra, *The Book of Secrets: Unlocking the Hidden Dimensions of Your Life* (New York: Harmony Books, 2004), 73-76.

10   Chief Leon Shenandoah, quoted in Andrew Harvey, *The Essential Mystics*, 6.

11   **Components of a greater wholeness**: Guy Murchie, ibid, 291-294.

11   **Fragmented consciousness**: Chopra, ibid, 120.

11   **Shifting our awareness**: Ken Wilber, *The Spectrum of Consciousness* (Wheaton, IL: Quest Books, 1993), 52-54.

11   Rabia of Basra, *Rabia of Basra: Selected Poems*, translated by Paul Smith (Victoria, Australia: New Humanity Books, 2016), 11.

12   Peter Russell, *From Science to God* (Novato, CA: New World Library, 2002), 79-82.

12   **Cause of suffering**: Chopra, ibid, 73, 82, 172, 219.

12   **Threefold nature**: Julio Savi, *The Eternal Quest for God: An Introduction to the Divine Philosophy of Abdu'l-Baha* (Oxford: George Ronald, 1989), 86.

13   Carl Jung, *Psychological Reflections*, ibid, 172.

13   Black Elk, quoted in J.G. Neihardt, *Black Elk Speaks* (Lincoln: University of Nebraska Press, 1961), 42-43.

14   **Power of insight**: Abdu'l-Baha, *Paris Talks: Addresses Given by Abdu'l-Baha in 1911* (Wilmette, IL: Baha'i Publishing Trust, 2006), 173-5.

14   **Seek and ye shall find**: Quoted in Jeffrey Moses, *Oneness: Great Principles Shared by All Religions* (New York: Ballantine Books, 2002), 91-93. (Matthew 7:7; Deuteronomy 4:29; Hadith no. 1, Abu Dharr al-Ghifari; Mishkat al-Masabih of Aliuddin Abu Abdullah Mahmud Al-Tabriza.

14   Shankara, quoted in Aldous Huxley, *The Perennial Philosophy*, ibid, 5.

14   Abdu'l-Baha, *Foundations of World Unity* (Wilmette, IL: Baha'i Publishing Trust, 1979), 15, 76.

14   **Human rights**: Baha'i International Community, "Development, Democracy, and Human Rights, Statement to the United Nations World Conference on Human Rights, 1993; Baha'i International Community, "Valuing Spirituality in Development: Initial Considerations Regarding the

Creation of Spiritually Based Indicators for Development." A Paper presented by the BIC to the meeting of religions and the World Bank, Lambeth Place, London, February 1998. http://www.bic.org

15   **Expanded consciousness**: Paul Lample, *Creating a New Mind* (Riviera Beach, FL: Palabra Publications, 1999), 3-7, 15-19.

15   Ervin Laszlo, *The Inner Limits of Mankind* (London: Oneworld, 1989), 65-67.

16   Deepak Chopra, ibid, 47-61.

16   Hildegard of Bingen, see http://www.azquotes.com/author/21274-Hildegard_of_Bingen

16   Wayne Teasdale, *The Mystic Heart*, 25-6, 101, 243.

2. ATTRACTION ALTERS THE COURSE OF CIVILIZATION

19   **Principle 2**: see Abdu'l-Baha, *Some Answered Questions,* 130; *Paris Talks,* 30; *Promulgation of Universal Peace,* 239; *Selected Writings of Abdu'l-Baha* (Haifa: Baha'i World Centre, 1978), 27-8.

21   William Blake, *The Complete Poems* (New York: Penguin Classics, 1977), 181.

21   *Rumi*, Ghazal, 1393, Tr. Nader Khalili.

21   **Awakening of love**: Nader Saiedi, *Logos and Civilization* (Bethesda: University Press of Maryland, 2000), 93, 103.

22   **One continuous moment**: Deepak Chopra, ibid, 198.

22   **Three forms of happiness**: Rhett Diessner, *Psyche and Eros: Baha'i Studies in a Spiritual Psychology* (Oxford: George Ronald, 2007), 158-160.

22   St. Catherine of Siena, *The Dialogue of St. Catherine of Siena: Seraphic Virgin and Doctor of Unity*, translated by Algar Thorold (Eremetical Press, 1907/2009), 17.

22   **Perpetual state**: Deepak Chopra, ibid, 217-223.

22   Mother Teresa, *No Greater Love* (Novato: New World Library, 2002), 29.

22   **Mother emotion**: Diessner, ibid, 160-163.

23   **In harmony**: Chopra, ibid, 25-27.

23   William James, *Memories and Studies* (Rockville, MD: Arc Manor, 2008), 84.

23   **Law of compassion**: C. Steven Evans, *Kierkegaard's Love Ethic: Divine Commands and Moral Obligations* (New York: Oxford University Press, 2004); Mark Spilka, *The Love Ethic of D.H. Lawrence* (Bloomington: Indiana University Press, 1955); M.L. King, Jr. *A Testament of Hope: The Essential Writings and Speeches of Martin Luther King, Jr.* (New York: HarperCollins, 1991); Cornel West, *Race Matters* (Boston: Beacon Press, 2001).

24   "The Creator's Gift," a traditional story as told by Phil Lane, Jr., quoted in Michael Bopp and Julie Bopp, *Recreating the World: A Practical Guide to Building Sustainable Communities* (Calgary, Alberta: Four Worlds Press, 2001), 88-89.

25   **Hardwired to connect**: A Report to the Nation from the Commission on Children at Risk, Executive Summary available online: www.americanvalues.org/html/hardwired.html

25   Einstein, quoted in Guy Murchie, *The Seven Mysteries of Life*, 513-515.

25   Jeremy Rifkin, *The Empathic Civilization: The Race to Global Consciousness in a World in Crisis* (New York: Tarcher, 2009).

26   **Virtues**: http://www.virtuesproject.com.

26   **Compassion   trigger**:   http://blogs.psychcentral.com/mindfulness/2010/01/what-everyone-should-know-about-the-mental-boost-from-altruism.

26   Tsunami aid: The Tsunami Evaluation Committee, consisting of UN agencies and other NGOs, described the aid commitments as the most generous and immediately funded (pdf) humanitarian response in history. Donations from individuals, businesses, trusts and foundations topped the list, accounting for half of total aid to the UN fund and making it the largest private response to any natural disaster.   https://www.theguardian.com/global-development/2014/dec/25/where-did-indian-ocean-tsunami-aid-money-go

26   **Reciprocal altruism**: Richard Wright, *Nonzero: The Logic of Human Destiny* (New York: Vintage, 2001), 22-24.

26   C.G. Jung, *Psychological Reflections* (Princeton: Princeton University Press, 1973), 38,42.

27   **More complex forms**: Robert Wright, *Nonzero*, 3-10, 107-108.

27   Baha'u'llah, *Gleanings*, 285.

28   **Four forces of nature**: William Hatcher, *Love, Power, and Justice* (Wilmette, IL: Baha'i Publishing Trust, 1998), 6-9, 23.

28   **Perpetual progress**: S. Bushrui and M. Massoudi, *The Spiritual Heritage of the Human Race* (Oxford: Oneworld, 2010), 110.

29   **The cause of unity**: Abdu'l-Baha, *The Promulgation of Universal Peace*, 394.

29   **Metta**: http://www.accesstoinsight.org/lib/authors/buddharakkhita/wheel365.html

29   **Supreme gift of love**: William Hatcher, ibid, 64-76.

30   **Spiritual values**: Nader Saiedi, *Logos and Civilization: Spirit, History, Order in the Writings of Baha'u'llah* (Bethesda: University Press of Maryland, 2000), 101-2.

30   **Distortions**: Universal House of Justice, *The Promise of World Peace: To the People's of the World* (Haifa: Baha'i World Centre, 1985, 2.

31-2   Rising tide... DNA... tribe of nomads: Peter Nichols, "The World Wanderers," *Penn Arts & Sciences*. Philadelphia: University of Pennsylvania, Fall/Winter 2008, 24-29.

32   **50th cousin**: Guy Murchie, ibid, 344-51.

33   Race: The Power of an Illusion, http://www.pbs.org/race

33   **A biological fiction**: Algernon Austin, "Race: Neither Biological Fact nor Social Fiction," *World Order* (Wilmette, IL: 2002, Vol. 33, No. 1), 9-20.

33   President   Obama   in   Dallas: https://www.whitehouse.gov/blog/2016/07/08/live-updates-attack-law-enforcement-dallas-texas

34   President   Obama   on   Japan: http://www.youtube.com/watch?v=7SrI6ebkZqI

34   **Principles of morality**: Abdu'l-Baha, *The Promulgation of Universal Peace*, 11-13.

34   **Love's celebration**: J. Redfield & M. Murphy, *God and the Evolving Universe: The Next Step in Personal Evolution* (New York: Tarcher, 2002), 121-3.

34   **Love is the safeguard**: See http://www.bahai.org/beliefs/essential-relationships/one-human-family/elimination-prejudice

34   Chief Joseph, quoted in Schaef, *Native Wisdom for White Minds*, March 2.

35   Baha'u'llah: See "The Elimination of Racial Discrimination," http://bic.org/statements-and-reports/statements/international-day-eliminate-racial-discrimination

35   Robert Wright, ibid, 294; see also, David Sloan Wilson, *Does Altruism Exist? Culture, Genes, and the Welfare of Others* (New Haven: Yale University Press, 2015).

35   **Universe is sustained**: Sai Ma, *Petals of Grace* (Boulder, CO: HIU Press, 2005), 3-6.

35   Pierre Teilhard de Chardin, *Activation of Energy* (New York: Harcourt, 1978), 70-1.

35   Abdu'l-Baha, *Selections from the Writings of Abdu'l-Baha*, 27.

3. CULTURE AND THE EVOLUTION OF JUSTICE

37   **Principle 3**: see Baha'u'llah, *The Seven Valleys and the Four Valleys*, 11; Baha'u'llah, *Gleanings*, 218-19; Baha'u'llah, *Tablets of Baha'u'llah*, (Wilmette, IL: Baha'i Publishing Trust, 1988), 66-8, 164; Abdu'l-Baha, *The Secret of Divine Civilization* (Wilmette, IL: Baha'i Publishing Trust, 1990), 69.

39   Martin Luther King, Jr., *The Papers of Martin Luther King, Jr.: Threshold of a New Decade, January 1959-December 1960* (Berkeley: University of California Press, 2005), 299.

39   Robert Wright, *Nonzero: The Logic of Human History*, 332.

39   **Greatest advancements**: Abdu'l-Baha, *The Promulgation of Universal Peace*, 12, 102.

40   **Moderation**: Baha'u'llah, *Gleanings*, 342.

40   Rose Pere, quoted in Schaef, *Native Wisdom for White Minds*, 12/4.

66   St. Catherine of Genoa, *Life and Doctrine of St. Catherine of Genoa*, edited by Paul A. Boer Sr. (Veritatis Splendor Publications/CreateSpace Platform, 2012), 227.

41   **Collective coming of age**: Baha'i International Community, *Who is Writing the Future? Reflections on the Twentieth Century* (New York: Office of Public Information, February, 1999).

41   Ken Wilber, "Breaking the Rules," in dialogue with Andrew Cohen,

What is Enlightenment? Magazine, Issue 22, Fall-Winter, 2002. Retrieved from http://www.wie.org/j22/gurupandit.asp?page=1.

41   Robert Wright, *Nonzero: The Logic of Human Destiny*, 5-7.

42   Baha'u'llah, *Gleanings from the Writings of Bahá'u'lláh*, 215.

42   **Conservatism and dynamism**: Barre Toelken, *The Dynamics of Folklore* (Boston: Houghton Mifflin, 1979), 34–43.

43   **Jihad vs. McWorld**: Wright, ibid, 202–04. See also Benjamin R. Barber, *Jihad vs. McWorld* (New York: Times Books/ Random House, 1995).

43   **Death pangs**: Shoghi Effendi, *The Promised Day Is Come* (Wilmette: Bahá'í Publishing Trust, 1980), 17.

44   **Mitakuye oyasin**: Schaef, *Native Wisdom for White Minds*, 3/30.

44   **Primal worldview**: Bushrui & Massoudi, *The Spiritual Heritage of the Human Race*, 40.

44   **Keepers of the earth**: Schaef, *Native Wisdom for White Minds*, 4/21.

45   **World unity**: Shoghi Effendi, *The World Order of Baha'u'llah* (Wilmette: Baha'i Publishing Trust, 1991), 202.

45   Upanishads, quoted in Andrew Harvey, *The Essential Mystics: Selections from the World's Great Wisdom Traditions* (New York: HarperCollins, 1997), 38-39.

46   **A world growing to maturity**: Shoghi Effendi, ibid.

46   For Abdu'l-Baha's discussion of inherent unity and intended unity see: *Selections from the Writings of Abdu'l-Baha*, 260-261, and *The Promulgation of Universal Peace*, 129-130.

46   **Unity in diversity**: See Baha'i International Community, *Valuing Spirituality in Development* (London: Baha'i Publishing Trust, 1998), 14-15; see also, Shoghi Effendi, *The World Order of Baha'u'llah*, 41-42.

47   **Moral responsibility**: See Shoghi Effendi, *The Advent of Divine Justice* (Wilmette: Baha'i Publishing Trust, 1990), 35; and, Baha'i International Community, *The Protection of Diversity in the Baha'i Community* (http://www.bahai.org/article-1-3-3-4.html).

47   Wilhelm Wundt, *Elements of Folk Psychology* (New York: Macmillan, 1912), especially 470-478.

48   Jolande Jacobi, *The Psychology of C.G. Jung* (New Haven: Yale, 1973), 8, 34-35.

48   Erik Erikson, "Remarks on the Wider Identity," in *A Way of Looking at Things: Selected Papers From 1930 to 1980*. (New York: Norton, 1986), p. 498, 499, 501.

49   **Golden Rule**: Jeffrey Moses, *Oneness: Great Principles Shared by All Religions* (New York: Ballantine Books, 2002), 5-7.

49   Baha'u'llah, *Tablets of Baha'u'llah* (Wilmette, IL: Baha'i Publishing Trust, 1988), 64.

50   **Deepest aspirations**: Moses, *Oneness*, 3.

51   Bono,   https://www.ted.com/talks/bono_s_call_to_action_for_africa?language=en

51   **Human rights approach**: Baha'i International Community's Submission to the United Nations High Commissioner for Human Rights regarding the draft "Guiding Principles on Human Rights and Extreme Poverty, BIC: New York, 1 September, 2007. http://www.bic.org/statements/guiding-principles-extreme-poverty-and-human-rights-0

51   **Structures of governance**: Sovaida Ma'ani Ewing, *Collective Security Within Reach* (Oxford: George Ronald, 2008), 3.

51   **Human capacity**: Holly Hanson, *A Path of Justice* (Secunderabad, India: Grace Publications, 2011), especially 103-122.

52   **The eye of oneness**: See Baha'u'llah, *The Hidden Words of Baha'u'llah* (Wilmette: Baha'i Publishing Trust, 1975), 3-4.

52   **A powerful force**: Baha'u'llah, *Tablets of Baha'u'llah*, 66-8; H. Hanson, *The Path of Justice*, 109.

53   **Web of interconnections**: James O'Dea, *Cultivating Peace: Becoming a 21st Century Peace Ambassador* (San Rafael, CA: Shift Books, 2012), 75.

53   **The fate of humanity**: see *Century of Light*, 134-5.

53   **Declaration**: Hans Kung, *A Global Ethic: The declaration of the Parliament of the World's Religions* (New York: Continuum, 1998), 14-15, 31.

4. OPPOSITION AS THE CATALYST FOR TRANSFORMATION

55   Abdu'l-Baha, *Selections from the Writings of Abdu'l-Baha*, 157; *The Promulgation of Universal Peace*, 140.

55   Mircea Eliade, *The Two and the One* (Chicago: University of Chicago Press, 1965), 120.

55   C.G. Jung, *Modern Man In Search of a Soul*, 211, 217.

57   **Principle 4**: see Baha'u'llah, *Gleanings,* 129; Baha'u'llah, *Prayers and Meditations by Baha'u'llah* (Wilmette, IL: Baha'i Publishing Trust, 1987), 155; Abdu'l-Baha, *Tablets of Abdu'l-Baha v3* (Wilmette, IL: Baha'i Publishing Trust, 1980), 513.

59   A.C. Swinburne, "Atalanta in Calydon," (1865) quoted in *The Great Thoughts*, George Seldes, compiler (New York: Ballantine Books, 1985), 404.

60   **Accelerating tide of change**: Gregory C. Dahl, *One World, One People* (Wilmette, Il: Baha'i Publishing, 2007), 25-26.

60   The Universal House of Justice, *The Promise of World Peace*, paragraph 11; *One Common Faith*, prepared under the supervision of The Universal House of Justice (Haifa: Baha'i World Centre, 2005), paragraph 1.

61   Plato, *The Republic*, Translated by F. M. Cornford (New York: Oxford University Press, 1951), 319.

61   **Something new appears**: Deepak Chopra, *The Book of Secrets*, 1-3, 108-110.

61   *Bhagavad-Gita*, translated by Edwin Arnold, XV, 16.

61   Heraclitus: Guy Murchie, *The Seven Mysteries of Life*, 471-2.

62-3   **Archetypes**: C.G. Jung, *Memories, Dreams, Reflections*, 392-3; see also, Jolande Jacobi, *The Psychology of C.G. Jung*, 47-49; Jolande Jacobi, *Complex Archetype Symbol in the Psychology of C.G. Jung* (Princeton: Princeton University Press, 1974), 31-73; and, June Singer, *Boundaries of the Soul*. New York: Anchor Books, 1994, 44, 100. For a more detailed discussion of myth, ritual, and archetype, and how their forms are all metaphors of transformation, see Robert Atkinson, *The Gift of Stories*, especially 25-47. See also, Jacobi, *The Psychology of C.G. Jung*, 67; C.G. Jung, "Archetypes of the Collective Unconscious," *The Archetypes of the Collective Unconscious*, 5, 28; C.G. Jung, *Psychological Reflections*, 1970, 38-39; Jolande Jacobi, *Complex Archetype Symbol*, 65; Anthony Storr, ed., *The Essential Jung* (Princeton: Princeton University Press, 1983), 16, 25.

63   **Rites of passage**: Arnold van Gennep, *The Rites of Passage*. Chicago (University of Chicago Press, 1909/1960).

63   Baha'u'llah, *Gleanings from the Writings of Baha'u'llah*, 129.

64   Abdu'l-Baha, *Tablets of Abdu'l-Baha*, *v3* (Wilmette, IL: Baha'i

Publishing Trust, 1980), 513; see also, John Hatcher, *Close Connections*, 101; and, Abdu'l-Baha, *The Promulgation of Universal Peace*, 172.

64   **Light and shadow**: Ruhiyyih Rabbani, *The Priceless Pearl* (London: Baha'i Publishing Trust, 1969), 118.

64   **Attributes of light**: Abdu'l-Baha, *Promulgation of Universal Peace*, 226; Baha'u'llah, *Kitab-i-Iqan/The Book of Certitude* (Wilmette, IL: Baha'i Publishing Trust, 1985), 142.

64   C.G. Jung, *Memories, Dreams, Reflections*, 398-9.

64   **The creative interrelationship**: Erich Neumann, *Depth Psychology and a New Ethic* (New York: Putnam, 1969), 143, 146-147.

65   **A conscious life**: Guy Murchie, ibid, 486-7.

65   C.G. Jung, *Memories, Dreams, Reflections*, 345, 311, 335; Jolande Jacobi, *The Psychology of C. G. Jung*, 53-55.

65   **Mistakes**: Schaef, *Native Wisdom for White Minds*, 3/27, 6/12.

65   Abdu'l-Baha, *Paris Talks* (London: Baha'i Publishing Trust, 1971), 178, 50-1.

66   See Mirabai Starr, translator, St. John of the Cross, *Dark Night of the Soul* (NY: Riverhead Books, 2003); and,Thomas Moore, *Dark Nights of the Soul* (New York: Gotham, 2004).

67   Paul Kennedy, *The Rise and Fall of Great Powers* (New York: Vintage, 1989).

99   Shoghi Effendi, *The World Order of Baha'u'llah*, 170.

67   *Crisis and Victory*. London: Baha'i Publishing Trust, 1988, iii, 36.

67   **Chaos the norm**: Hooper Dunbar, *Forces of Our Time* (Oxford: George Ronald, 2009), 45-50.

68   **Baha'i writings**: see *The Promise of World Peace*, para. 2, 6, 9 and 11; and, *Century of Light*, prepared under the supervision of The Universal House of Justice (Haifa: Baha'i World Centre, 2001), 139.

69   C.G. Jung, *Modern Man in Search of a Soul*, 217-19.

69   Pierre Teilhard de Chardin, Letter from Peking (Summer 1940), quoted in *The Last European War: September 1939/December 1941* (1976) by John Lukacs, p. 515

69   Ervin Laszlo, *Worldshift 2012: Making Green Business, New Politics, and Higher Consciousness Work Together* (Rochester, VT: Inner Traditions,

2009), ch.1; 99; 111.

70   Barbara Marx Hubbard, *Conscious Evolution: Awakening the Power of Our Social Potential* (Novato, CA: New World Library, 1998), 40.

70   Desmond Tutu and Mpho Tutu, *Made for Goodness: And Why This Makes All the Difference* (New York: HarperOne, 2010), 7.

70   James Redfield and Michael Murphy, *God and the Evolving Universe*, 21-75.

70   **Unifying vision**: Hooper Dunbar, *Forces of Our Time*, 46.

71   **A new consciousness of oneness**: www.bahai.org.

72   Baha'u'llah, quoted in Shoghi Effendi, *The World Order of Baha'u'llah*, 25.

5. SPIRITUAL FORCES GUIDING US TOWARD UNITY

73   Abdu'l-Baha, *The Promulgation of Universal Peace*, 372.

73   Julian of Norwich, *All Will Be Well*, edited by John Kirvan (Notre Dame, IN: Ave Maria Press, 2008), 81.

73   Albert Einstein, *The Quotable Einstein*. Ed., A. Calaprice (Princeton: Princeton University Press, 1966), 199.

75   **Principle 5**: see, Abdu'l-Baha, *ibid.*; Abdu'l-Baha, *Foundations of World Unity*, 29; *Baha'u'llah*, a Statement prepared by the Baha'i International Community (New York: BIC, 1992), 17; The Universal House of Justice, *The Promise of World Peace*; Hooper Dunbar, *Forces of Our Time*, 52.

77   Paul Carus, *The Gospel of Buddha* (Chicago: Open Court Publishing, 1915), 142.

77   Martin Buber, *The Way of Response: Selected Writings* (New York: Schocken Books, 1966), 29.

77   David Bohm, quoted in Michael Talbot, *The Holographic Universe*, 60-1.

77   **Same unified reality**: Mircea Eliade, *The Two and the One* (Chicago: University of Chicago Press, 1979), 78-124.

78   **Physical world an expression of spirit**: Hooper Dunbar, *Forces of Our Time*, 6.

78   Johanna Macy, *Consciousness and Healing*, 530.

78   Deepak Chopra, *The Book of Secrets*, 35.

79   **Divine truth is relative**: Shoghi Effendi, *The World Order of Bahá'u'lláh*, 58.

79   **Visualize the consciousness continuum**: for chart and description, see Robert Atkinson, "Which Way Humanity? Reflections on the Peace/War Continuum," *The Maine Scholar*, Vol. 16, Winter, 2004.

81   **Achieving oneness**: Bushrui, ibid, 108.

115   **Tawhid**: Geoffrey Parrinder, *Mysticism in the World's Religions* (Oxford: Oneworld, 1995), 15.

81   **From duality to unity**: Deepak Chopra, *The Book of Secrets*, 105-6; D. Chopra, *How to Know God: The Soul's Journey Into the Mystery of Mysteries* (New York: Three Rivers Press, 2000), 113-5, 176-8.

82   Bahá'u'lláh, *The Seven Valleys and the Four Valleys*, 17, 24-5.

82   **Circle of love**: Moses, *Oneness*, ibid, 8-11, 52-55.

82   Bahá'u'lláh, quoted in Shoghi Effendi, *The Promised Day is Come* (Wilmette, IL: Baha'i Publishing, 1996), 190-2.

83   Chief Seattle, quoted in Kathleen Brehony, *Living A Connected Life* (New York: Henry Holt, 2003), 129.

83   Ervin Laszlo, *The Connectivity Hypothesis: Foundations of an Integral Science of Quantum, Cosmos, and Consciousness* (Albany: SUNY Press, 2000), vii-viii, 49-79, 103-118.

83   Lynn McTaggart, *The Field: The Quest For the Secret Force of the Universe* (New York: HarperCollins, 2008), xx.

83   Paul Davies, *The Cosmic Blueprint: New Discoveries in Nature's Creative Ability to Order the Universe* (West Conshohocken, PA: Templeton Foundation Press, 2004), xvi, 8.

83   Deepak Chopra, *How to Know God*, 68, 177; Chopra, *Book of Secrets*, 22-44.

83   Wayne Teasdale, ibid., 23.

84   Desmond Tutu, *God Has a Dream: A Vision of Hope for Our Time* (New York: Image Doubleday, 2004).

85   **A new eye**: Bahá'u'lláh, *Gleanings*, 267.

85   Ralph Waldo Emerson, *Essays: First Series* (Stilwell, KS: Digireads. com Publishing, 2007), 5, 84.

86   Larry Dossey, *One Mind: How Our Individual Mind Is Part of a*

Greater Consciousness and Why It Matters (Carlsbad, CA: Hay House, 2013), xxviii.

86   Baha'i International Community, *World Citizenship: A Global Ethic for Sustainable Development* (New York, statement issued June 14, 1993). http://statements.bahai.org/93-0614.htm

86   Winona LaDuke, http://www.azquotes.com/author/19248-Winona_LaDuke

87   **Unity a condition of the human spirit**: *Century of Light*, 41, 143-4; *One Common Faith*, 42-3, 55.

87-8   **Flowers of a garden... world unity**: Shoghi Effendi, *The World Order of Baha'u'llah*, 41-42; Baha'i International Community, *The Prosperity of Humankind* (Haifa: Baha'i World Center, 1995), 4; Shoghi Effendi, *The World Order of Baha'u'llah*, 202.

88   Pierre Teilhard de Chardin, *The Human Phenomenon*, ibid., 3.

88   Arnold Toynbee, quoted in Peter Russell, *From Science to God*, 123.

88   Joseph Campbell, *The Masks of God: Creative Mythology* (New York: Viking, 1968), xx.

88   David Bohm, quoted in Lynn McTaggart, *The Field*, xxiii-xxiv.

89   **UN Millennium Summit**: Quoted in *Century of Light*, 129-36.

89   Baha'u'llah, *Gleanings*, 286.

89   **Peace as inevitable**: see, The Universal House of Justice, *The Promise of World Peace*; Hooper Dunbar, *Forces of Our Time*, 52.

89   **The great religions**: *One Common Faith*, 13-4, 22.

90   Evelyn Underhill, *Mysticism*, 173.

90   Baha'u'llah, *Gleanings*, 213.

90   **transformative energies**: *One Common Faith*, 14; Hooper Dunbar, ibid, vii.

6. THE MYSTERY OF DIVINITY

93   **Principle 6**: see, Baha'u'llah, *Gleanings*, 74-5; Abdu'l-Baha, *The Promulgation of Universal Peace*, 140-3, 198, 378; Shoghi Effendi, *The Promised Day is Come*, v; Shoghi Effendi, *The World Order of Baha'u'llah*, 58; Baha'i International Community, *One Common Faith*, 22-3.

95   Tolstoy, quoted in John Huddleston, *The Earth Is But One Country*

(Wilmette, IL: Baha'i Publishing Trust, 1976), 27, from *Star of the West*, Vol. xxiii, 233.

95   Abdu'l-Baha, *Some Answered Questions*, 199.

95   The Torah, Exodus 3:13

96   Baha'u'llah, *Gleanings*, 63.

96   **Openness to the divine**: Suheil Bushrui, *The Spiritual Heritage of the Human Race*, 6, 23-4.

97   **The Story of the Sacred Tree**: http://www.fwii.net/profiles/blogs/the-story-of-the-sacred-tree.

97   **The Peacemaker**: https://nnidatabase.org/video/oren-lyons-looking-toward-seventh-generation.

97   **Principles of Native spirituality**: Joel Beversluis, ed., *Sourcebook of the World's Religions* (Novato, CA: New World Library, 2000), 48.

97   Black Elk, *The Sacred Pipe: Black Elk's Account of the Seven Rites of the Oglala Sioux* (New York: Penguin, 1980), xx; see also Moses, *Oneness, 120*; Scheaf, *Native Wisdom for White Minds*, 2/1.

97   **Religion as a single tree**: John Hatcher, *The Face of God Among Us*, 11-12. See also, http://en.wikipedia.org/wiki/Religion; http://en.wikipedia.org/wiki/Abrahamic_religions; http://en.wikipedia.org/wiki/Indian_religions; Ruhiyyih Rabbani, *The Priceless Pearl*, ibid, 372.

98   Abdu'l-Baha, *The Promulgation of Universal Peace*, 198.

98   **Divine truth as relative**: Shoghi Effendi, *The World Order of Baha'u'llah*, 58.

98   **Continuing nature**: *The Bhagavad Gita*. Translated by Eknath Easwaran (Berkeley: Nilgiri Press, 2007), 119; Isaiah, 62.2.

98   Buddha, quoted in Paul Carus, *The Gospel of Buddha*, 217.

98-9   Christ... Muhammad: John 16: 12-13; Qur'an 11:105; 13:39.

99   Baha'u'llah quoted in Druzelle Cederquist, *The Story of Baha'u'llah: Promised One of All Religions* (Wilmette, IL: Baha'i Publishing, 2005), 163.

99   Rumi, *Look! This is Love – Poems of Rumi*, Translated by Annemarie Schimmel (Boston: Shambhala, 1991).

99   **Misconceptions**: *One Common Faith* (Haifa: Baha'i World Center, 2005), 18-9.

99   Abdu'l-Baha, *The Promulgation of Universal Peace*, 140.

100   **One universal law**: *One Common Faith*, 20-1.

100   Pierre Teilhard de Chardin, *The Phenomenon of Man*, ibid.

100   **The purpose**: *One Common Faith*, 22.

101   **Recast religion**: *One Common Faith*, 22-3.

101   Baha'u'llah, *Gleanings*, 136.

101   **A new chapter begins**: *Century of Light*, 137.

102   Baha'u'llah, ibid, 137-8; *Prayers and Meditations* (Wilmette, IL: Baha'i Publishing Trust, 1998), 295.

102   Deepak Chopra, *How To Know God*, 4-6.

103   **A new spiritual feast**: *One Common Faith*, 18-24. This concept of a single Reality being illustrated as a "sandwich" is also represented in the Baha'i ringstone symbol. http://bahaiteachings.org/what-do-the-bahai-symbols-mean

103   Baha'u'llah, *Gleanings*, 287-9.

103   **A pervasive spiritual energy**: Hooper Dunbar, *Forces of Our Time*, 8-9, 12-14.

103   **Primary objective**: Office of Public Information, *Baha'u'llah* (New York: Baha'i International Community, 1991), 12-28.

103   **Progressive revelation**: Nader Saiedi, *Logos and Civilization*, 9, 11.

103   Shoghi Effendi, *The Promised Day is Come*, v.

104   **Distinguishing feature**: Shoghi Effendi, ibid, 122-26.

105   **Spiritual precepts**: see, http://www.bahai.org; Baha'u'llah, *Tablets of Baha'u'llah* (Wilmette, IL: Baha'i Publishing Trust, 1988), 142; *One Common Faith*, 40; *Century of Light*, 1, 90, 128; Suheil Bushrui, *Retrieving Our Spiritual Heritage* (Wilmette, IL: Baha'i Publishing, 2012), especially Chapter 1, "Retrieving Our Spiritual Heritage: A Challenge of Our Time," and Chapter 8, "Environmental Ethics: A Baha'i Perspective." The Baha'i International Community also contributed an official statement, titled "Shared Vision, Shared Volition: Choosing Our Global Future Together," to the UN Conference on Climate Change in Paris in 2015 (COP21), which emphasized how the principle of the oneness of humanity recasts the whole concept of relationships for a sustainable planet, and called for collective action on issues of sustainability: https://www.bic.org/statements/shared-vision-shared-volition-choosing-our-global-future-together#PDgFBI6WKQtYI3Kw.97

107   **An all-embracing vision**: *One Common Faith*, 38-41.

107   Tahirih (Qurratu'l-Ayn) quoted in Margaret Smith, *Rabi'a The Mystic and Her Fellow-Saints in Islam* (New York: Cambridge University Press, 2010), 162; see also, https://en.m.wikipedia.org/wiki/Táhirih.

108   Samuel P. Huntington, *The Clash of Civilizations and the Remaking of World Order* (New York: Simon & Schuster, 2011), 320.

108   Baha'u'llah, *Gleanings*, 250, 334.

108   Hans Kung, *A Global Ethic*, 17-35.

108   **Sciences confirm**: See *The Promise of World Peace*, http://info.bahai.org/article-1-7-2-1.html.

109   Ervin Laszlo, *The Inner Limits of Mankind: Heretical Reflections on Today's Values, Culture and Politics* (Oxford: Oneworld Publications, 1989), 65-67, 120-28.

7. THE INHERENT HARMONY OF REASON AND FAITH

113   **Principle 7**: see Abdu'l-Baha, *The Promulgation of Universal Peace*, 63, 66, 107, 128, 231, 394; Abdu'l-Baha, *Paris Talks*, 141-6; Abdu'l-Baha, *Some Answered Questions*, 3, 182.

115   Charles Darwin, *The Descent of Man*. New York: Penguin Classics, 2004, 147.

115   Alfred North Whitehead, quoted in Huston Smith, *Why Religion Matters: The Fate of the Human Spirit in an Age of Disbelief* (New York: HarperCollins, 2001), 73.

115   Edgar Mitchell, quoted in Marilyn Schlitz and Tina Amorok (eds.) *Consciousness & Healing: Integral Approaches to Mind-Body Medicine* (St. Louis: Elsevier, 2005), xiii.

116   **Trend of evolution**: Guy Murchie, *The Seven Mysteries of Life*, 513-4.

116   David Sloan Wilson, see also http://interspirituality.com/altruism.

117   Charles Darwin, ibid.

117   **Ethic of reciprocity**: Guy Murchie, ibid, 514.

117   **Impulse toward altruism**: Scott Hunt, *The Future of Peace: On the Front Lines With the World's Greatest Peacemakers* (New York: HarperOne, 2004), 338.

118   Darwin quoted by Watson & Crick, in *National Geographic Magazine*,

February, 2009.

118   Einstein quoted in Murchie, ibid, 514.

118   Charles Darwin, *The Origin of Species* (New York: Bantam Classics, 1999), 489.

119   **Perfections appear by degrees**: Abdu'l-Baha, *Some Answered Questions*, 198-9.

119   **Perennial philosophy**: Quoted in Geoffrey Moses, *Oneness: Great Principles Shared By All Religions*, 14; and, Aldous Huxley, *The Perennial Philosophy*, 8.

119   The grand synthesis: Ervin Laszlo, *Evolution: The Grand Synthesis* (Boston: Shambhala Publications, 1992).

119   **More similarities**: Guy Murchie, ibid, 612-3.

120   Rumi, *The Rumi Collection: An Anthology of Translations* (Boston: Shambhala, 2005) 112.

120   **Two wings**: Abdu'l-Baha, *The Promulgation of Universal Peace*, 11-13; 63-64; 181.

120   Abdu'l-Baha, Ibid, 231.

120   Albert Einstein, *The Einstein Reader* (New York: Citadel, 2003), 23.

121   Pierre Teilhard de Chardin, *Science and Christ* (New York: Harper & Row, 1965), 83.

121   Paul Davies, *The Mind of God: The Scientific Basis for a Rational World* (New York: Simon & Schuster, 1993).

121   Peter Russell, *From Science to God* (Novato, CA: New World Library, 2002), chapter 8.

Consciousness & Healing, p. 357.

121   David Bohm quoted in Lynn McTaggart, ibid, xxv.

121   Max Planck quoted in Gregg Braden, *The Divine Matrix: Bridging Time, Space, Miracles, and Belief* (Carlsbad, CA: Hay House, 2008), 3.

122   Einstein quoted in Murchie, ibid, 610.

122   Charles Darwin, *The Origin of Species*, 132.

122   **The utterance**: Baha'u'llah, *Gleanings*, 288.

122   **Ye dwell**: Baha'u'llah, *Gleanings*, 334; *Tablets of Baha'u'llah* (Wilmette, IL: Baha'i Publishing Trust, 1995), 130.

122   **This endless universe:** Abdu'l-Baha, *Some Answered Questions* (2014

edition), Section 69, para. 3.

122   **All phenomena**: Abdu'l-Baha, *The Promulgation of Universal Peace*, 286.

123   **Brian   Swimme**:   http://www.azquotes.com/author/43588-Brian_ Swimme.

123   Ervin Laszlo, *Evolution: The Grand Synthesis* (Boston: Shambhala, 1987).

123   **We exist as a unity**: Lynn McTaggart, *The Field*, xx-xxiii.

123   **The primary principle**: www.bahai.org.

123   **The goal**: Office of Public Information, *Baha'u'llah*, 25.

124   **An interfaith movement**: For a brief and mostly balanced history of the first Parliament and beyond, see Karl-Josef Kuschel, "The Parliament of the World's Religions, 1893-1993" in Hans Kung, *A Global Ethic*, ibid, 77-105; see also, Rev. Dr. Marcus Braybrooke, "The Interfaith Movement of the 20th Century," in Beversluis, *Sourcebook of the World's Religions*, 129-137.

124   **World Council of Churches**: Robert Stockman, "The Baha'i Faith and Interfaith Relations," *World Order* (Wilmette, IL.: Baha'i Publishing, 2002), Summer, 19-21.

124   **World Congress of Faiths**: http://www.worldfaiths.org/index.php

125   http://templeofunderstanding.org

125   **Immigration Act…**: Robert Stockman, ibid, 21.

125   Wayne Teasdale, *The Mystic Heart*, 9.

125   **United Religions Initiative**: http://www.uri.org

126   Teasdale, *ibid*, xvii, 4-6, 10, 26-7, 163, 236, 239.

126   Kurt Johnson: http://www.thecominginterspiritualage.com; http:// interspirituality.com; http://multiplex.isdna.org/declaration.htm

127   http://www.interfaithpowerandlight.org

127   https://www.ifyc.org

127   http://universalhouseofjustice.bahai.org/involvement-life-society/20020401_001

129   **Indigenous voices… visions**: Bette Stockbauer, "Ancient Prophesies for Modern Times," in Beversluis, *Sourcebook of the World's Religions*, 45-49.

131   **Our collective coming of age**: Baha'i International Community, *One Common Faith*, 53-56.

131   Oren Lyons quoted in Steven McFadden, *Legend of the Rainbow Warriors* (New York: Harlem Writers Guild, 2005), 80.

EPILOGUE:

133   Desmond Tutu and Mpho Tutu, *Made For Goodness*, x, 5, 7, 43.

133   Rachel Carson, *Silent Spring* (New York: Houghton Mifflin, 1962), 277.

133   Barbara Marx Hubbard, "Conscious Evolutionaries: A New Breed of Global Citizen," *Shift: At the Frontiers of Consciousness*, September-November, 2004, 28-31.

134   *More alike*: Maya Angelou, "Human Family," *I Shall Not Be Moved* (NY: Knopf, 1990).

134   **Change of consciousness**: *Century of Light*, 136.

135   Ervin Laszlo, *Worldshift 2012*, 98, 110-11.

135   Martin Luther King, Jr., *A Call to Conscience: The Landmark Speeches of Dr. Martin Luther King, Jr.*, Clay Carson and Kris Shepard, eds. (New York: Warner Books, 2001), 160-61.

135   **Spiritual forces**: Shoghi Effendi, *The World Order of Baha'u'llah*, 16-17, 22-26.

135   James O'Dea, *Cultivating Peace*, especially chapters 9 & 10.

135   Barbara Marx Hubbard, *Birth 2012 and Beyond: Humanity's Great Shift to the Age of Conscious Evolution* (San Rafael, CA: Shift Books, 2012).

136   **Champions of justice**: Paul Lample, *Creating a New Mind*, 4-5.

136   **Groups and movements**: for an extensive directory and listing of interfaith, multi-faith, and inter-religious organizations of all kinds, see Beversluis, *Sourcebook of the World's Religions*, 355-430.

140   Desmond Tutu and Mpho Tutu, *Made for Goodness*, 116.

140   **Better mutual understanding**: Hans Kung, *A Global Ethic*, 36.

APPENDIX I

141   Sources consulted to compile this timeline include: Bushrui & Massoudi, *The Spiritual Heritage of the Human Race*, ibid.; Redfield & Murphy, *God and the Evolving Universe*, ibid.; and, J. Moses, *Oneness*, ibid.

APPENDIX II

153   Sources consulted for this meditation include: Philip Novak, *The World's Wisdom: Sacred Texts of the World's Religions* (New York: Harper Collins, 1995) Chapter 2, Buddhism, pp.71-4; and Baha'u'llah, *The Seven Valleys and the Four Valleys.*

Index

principle, x, xiii-xvi, xviii, 14, 28, 30, 35, 46, 49-52, 68, 70-2, 78-81, 87-8, 90-1, 101, 103, 104-5, 107-9, 117-8, 120, 122, 123, 127, 130, 134-5, 136, 138, 146;
   of inevitable progress, vi, 146
progress, ii, v-vi, x, xiii, xiv, xvii, 28, 31, 35, 39-40, 57, 64, 67, 69, 71-2, 79, 84, 87-9, 93, 109, 119, 122-3, 134
Prophets/Messengers (of God), i, 14, 34, 71, 78, 82, 93, 96-9, 102-3, 106, 109, 118, 120, 123, 129, 144
"promised day," v, 75, 130

Q
Quantum theory, 78, 83, 88, 121, 123, 149, 150
quest, xi, 5-8, 13, 14, 16, 17, 29, 63, 95, 115
Qur'an, 64, 104, 130, 144

R
Rabia of Basra, 11, 144
race, iii, 31-4;
   as an illusion, 33;
   as biological fiction, 33;
   as social construction, 33
racism, 32, 34, 40, 45, 79-80, 90, 106, 136
Reality, i-ii, x, xiii-xv, 1, 7, 12, 16, 57, 60, 96, 138, 142
   continuum, 78-81;
   investigation of, xi, 3, 9, 11, 15, 71, 105;
   is one, 10, 14, 23, 30, 64, 73, 75, 77, 82-4, 88, 98, 100-1, 106, 109-10, 113, 116, 119-20, 126, 134;
   sandwich, 102-3, 123
Redfield, James, 70
rebirth, i, v, 61, 66-8, 70-1, 75, 102
Red Cross, 31
religion, i, xi, xiii, xv-xvii, 28, 31, 34, 44, 48, 70-1, 81, 89, 95, 98, 105, 108, 124, 129;
   all agree, 8-9, 14-5, 25, 50, 53, 62,

78, 84, 103, 110, 123, 126;
   evolving, xivv, 96, 99-101, 104, 109, 127;
   future prophesies of, 129;
   tree of, 96-8
renewal, i-ii, v-vi, xviii, 9, 68, 72, 85, 98, 102, 146
resolution, vi, viii, 66
revelation, ii, xiii, xvi, 49-50, 62, 70-2, 82, 89, 103-4, 116, 119, 122-3, 128, 130, 135, 141, 142, 144, 146;
   progressive, xiii, 93, 96, 98-9, 100-1, 102, 120
Rifkin, Jeremy, 25
rites of passage, 61, 63
Royal Humane Society, 31, 145
Rumi, 4, 6, 21-3, 99, 120, 144
Russell, Peter, 12, 121

S
sacred traditions, xiv-xv, 17, 49, 52, 64, 75, 96-7, 117, 122-4, 129
sacred stories, vi, 61
Salvation Army, 31, 145
science, great teachers of, 120
science and religion, 71, 100, 105, 110, 113, 115-6, 118-21, 123, 134, 145-7
scientific truth as relative, 32, 79
Seattle, Chief, 83
Seeger, Pete, xi
service to humanity, 107, 124, 136, 139-40, 143, 156
shadow, 26, 59, 64-5
Shankara, 6, 14, 145
Shenandoah, Chief Leon, 10
Shintoism, 119
Shoghi Effendi, xvi, 67, 88, 103
Sikh tradition, 97, 125, 138, 145
soul, x-xi, 4, 9, 12, 22, 23, 39, 52, 85, 87, 139, 154, 156;
   dark night of, 66-8;
   journey of, xii, 8, 14, 35, 81
spiritual, i-iii, v, xii, xv-xvi, 8, 12, 16, 21, 43, 66, 84, 96, 122;

Whitman, Walt, 5
wholeness, xiv-xv, 11, 23, 42, 46, 52-3, 64, 67, 77-81, 84, 88, 113, 119, 121, 131, 133
Wilber, Ken, 41
Women's Rights Movement, 33, 146
Word, the, 101-2
world/global citizen, 46, 80, 85-6, 108, 110, 135-6
world peace, xiii, 15, 50, 52, 68-9, 71, 75, 80, 87, 89-90, 105-6, 108, 122, 126, 130, 135, 137-8, 148, 150
world unity, xvii, 45, 47, 53-4, 75, 87-90, 102, 105-6, 108, 111, 123, 128, 130, 139
World Congress of Faiths, 124, 149
Wright, Robert, 35, 39, 41-2
Wundt, Wilhelm, 47-8, 148

Y
Yin-Yang, 62, 120, 142
yoga, 6, 15, 17, 81, 97

Z
Zoroaster, i, 97, 99, 100, 142

About the Author

Robert Atkinson, Ph.D., is an internationally acknowledged authority on life story interviewing and a pioneer in the deeper techniques of personal mythmaking and soul-making. His books in these areas have been translated in to three languages and are widely used in personal growth and life review settings.

His most recent book, Mystic Journey: Getting to the Heart of Your Soul's Story (2012), was called "an exquisite exploration of the spiritual craft of soul-making" by Jean Houston, author of A Mythic Life. Of his memoir, Remembering 1969: Searching for the Eternal in Changing Times (2008), Thomas Moore, author of Care of the Soul, said it was "profound, friendly, inspiring, and nostalgic… I loved it."

His other books include, Songs of the Open Road: The Poetry of Folk Rock and the Journey of the Hero (1974); The Teenage World: Adolescents'

Self-Image in Ten Countries (1987); The Gift of Stories: Practical and Spiritual Applications of Autobiography, Life Stories, and Personal Mythmaking (1995; translated into Japanese, 2005); The Life Story Interview (1998; translated into Italian, 2002, and Romanian, 2006); The Beat of My Drum (2005), an autobiography with Babatunde Olatunji; and, Latino Voices in New England (2009).

His BA is in Philosophy and American Studies from LIU, Southampton, and his MA degrees are in American Folk Culture from SUNY, Cooperstown, and in Counseling from the University of New Hampshire. His Ph.D. is in Cross-Cultural Human Development from the University of Pennsylvania; he was also a post-doctoral research fellow at the University of Chicago.

At the University of Southern Maine, he was the first Diversity Scholar in the College of Education and Human Development, and a co-founding faculty of the Russell Scholars Program and the Religious Studies minor. He was also a faculty member on the fall 2002 Semester at Sea voyage around the world. He is professor emeritus at USM, and director of Story Commons. www.robertatkinson.net.

CPSIA information can be obtained
at www.ICGtesting.com
Printed in the USA
FSHW02n0423280818
51605FS